Rails in the North Woods

Richard S. Allen
William Gove
Keith F. Maloney
Richard F. Palmer

Drawings by
John D. Mahaffy

Rails in the North Woods

NORTH COUNTRY BOOKS
Utica, New York

RAILS IN THE NORTH WOODS
Copyright © 1978

NORTH COUNTRY BOOKS

ISBN 0-925168-69-6

Second Revised Edition
First Paperback
1999

Frontispiece courtesy of Katharine Virkler

NORTH COUNTRY BOOKS
311 Turner Street
Utica, New York 13501

ABOUT THE AUTHORS

RICHARD S. ALLEN

A native of Saratoga Springs, writer/compiler Richard Sanders Allen has had a life-long interest in the history of New York State.

A freelance researcher, Allen is a past consultant to the Penfield Foundation, the Mobil Travel Guide, the National Park Service, and the Smithsonian Institution in Washington, D.C. He has prepared historical surveys of over a dozen New York State counties for the New York State Historic Trust and was also involved with the planning of the New York State Museum in Albany.

Allen was the recipient of a Guggenheim Fellowship in 1962, and has authored several books and numerous articles devoted to covered wooden bridges, early iron manufacture, and airplanes of the 1930s.

For a decade he served as program and then executive director of New York State's American Revolution Bicentennial Commission. Since his retirement, he has been a recipient of the American Society of Civil Engineers' History and Heritage Award.

Allen is currently engaged in a study of structures on the abandoned right-of-way of the Milwaukee Railroad.

He lives in Lewiston, Idaho.

WILLIAM GOVE

William "Bill" Gove is a retired forester who has been an active fan of lumbering and railroading history for over thirty-five years.

He is a native of Maine, and a graduate of the University of Maine with a B.S. in forestry. He worked in the sawmill and plywood industries before pursuing a career with the Vermont Department of Forests and Parks as a wood utilization specialist.

Gove has researched and recorded the histories of all of the logging railroads of New England as well as those in other regions of the Northeast. He has authored a number of books and magazine articles with a desire to record the past and the influence of lumbering and railroading on modern society.

He maintains his retirement home in Vermont.

RICHARD F. PALMER

Born in Canandaigua, New York, Richard Palmer has had a keen interest in railroading since childhood. He grew up next to the main line of the New York Central in Palmyra in the days of steam, and spent many hours watching trains with his father.

High school years were spent on a farm near Fulton, New York, with spare moments spent watching the nearby New York, Ontario & Western during the final years of its existence. He has subsequently been a newspaper reporter.

He is a member of the National Railway Historical Society and several other historical organizations. Through the years he had written numerous articles and books on now-abandoned rail lines in upstate New York.

He is also active in the Great Lakes Historical Society, and is particularly interested in Lake Ontario's maritime history. He had written many articles for that group's quarterly publication, "Inland Seas." He is currently the editor of the *Baldwinsville Messenger* in Baldwinsville, New York.

The Palmers live in the Syracuse area.

KEITH F. MALONEY

Keith F. Maloney became fascinated with the rail scene as a child while living in the hamlet of Buffalo Head, New York, also known as Forestport Station on the old M&M/ Adirondack Railroad.

While in high school at Beaver Falls, New York, he became interested in the rail hobby when the aging No. 1923 steam locomotive was temporarily reactivated on the Lowville & Beaver River, which ran only a few hundred yards from his parents' home.

For the past thirty-five years Maloney has been active in various phases of journalism. He had been a reporter for the *Watertown Daily Times* and the *Syracuse Post-Standard*, a publications and advertising writer for several companies, and has also been involved with newspaper editing, graphic arts, and printing. More recently he has worked in advertising sales and has served as publications director for a large evangelical church in Syracuse.

In 1989 he became acquainted with Livingston Lansing, well-known businessman and developer from Boonville, New York, and helped influence Lansing to investigate operating his Shay locomotive on the Lowville & Beaver River.

TABLE OF CONTENTS

PREFACE

In the early years of the nineteenth century, as in the 1870's, New York State saw a period of rapid railroad development. Times have changed and tree-grown cuts and fills, weed-smothered embankments wandering apparently aimlessly up quiet valleys bear mute testimony to the drive and dreams of a legion of forgotten men who built them, hoping to bring progress to their communities and wealth to themselves.

Hardly a town of any consequence escaped railroad fever. Some, with their attendant bands of steel, reached affluence and the status of cities. Most spurted for a time, got caught up in the excitement of a burgeoning nation, then relaxed into drowsy contemplation of what might have been.

Generally, the life of a short line has depended upon one or two industries, in many cases the principal customer owning the majority of the stock.

The builders of short lines were civic leaders and promoters, not economists. Theirs was simply the fire of financial gain, fanned by a fever that swept the country like a ravaging plague. Railroad fever has left its scars.

This is the story of a handful of short lines, only one of which exists today, for the life of a short line railroad has always been precarious.

Cited in this work are several examples of short lines which are considered typical of New York State. Two were built strictly for mining, two for lumbering, and two for general commodities. Of these, only one remains today—the Lowville & Beaver River Railroad.

Broad ribbons of macadam and concrete penetrate the lush valleys today, often parallel with the deserted embankments which sometimes, it seems, in lonely discouragement, remove themselves from the speeding motorists to wander off through the meadows to the hills.

Occasionally there is a faded station, likely living out its days beside the trackless grade as a storage shed for farm machinery or some other equally plebeian adjunct to modern rural living.

Recent emphasis upon the quality of the environment may swing the pendulum in favor of the railroads. It has been pointed out that one or two diesel engines can haul a load of cargo equal to the efforts of many trucks and with much less pollution of the air. The railroad was a vital element in the building of our nation in the past, and may be an even greater factor in the industrial life and transportation of the future.

This book is a joint effort by several people, namely, Richard Allen, William Gove, Keith Maloney, and myself. All have devoted many hours in extensive research, accumulating materials, and writing. It is felt this work represents a cross-section of short line railroading in northern New York State.

—RICHARD PALMER

ACKNOWLEDGEMENTS

The authors wish to thank all those who have helped to make the writing of this book possible. A special thanks goes to Roy Sykes, Loren Silliman, the George Sykes family, Keith Hamele, Victor Noelk, Phil Haddock, and Frank Reed.

Gratitude is also extended to Pat McKenney, Paul Thomas, Margaret Lansing, Mrs. John Olson, Margaret Witherell, Floyd Horth, Philip Hastings, Ray Zenger, and Thomas T. Taber III.

Peter E. Gores, Ed Schnabl, Livingston Lansing, David J. Monte Verde, Urban Karcher, Christina Balash, and Maurice Switzer were invaluable contributors during the research for this book, as were the magazines *Railpace Newsmagazine*, *Railroad Model Craftsman*, and the Lowville *Journal & Republican*.

To those who may have been inadvertently omitted from this acknowledgement, we are also truly grateful.

The Rich Lumber Company

by William Gove

Among the earliest of rails to stretch through the north woods were those of the logger, that stalwart of the Adirondacks. The north country of northeastern New York has always possessed a wealth of forest resources to beckon the lumberman. And be it from the hillside abode of the stately spruce and majestic pine, or the lowland home of the ponderous maple, the logger found a way out for his cumbersome logs.

The Adirondacks were opened to full-scale logging rather late in the history of land development and exploitation. Pennsylvania had received the embraces of the logger much earlier, but when the "old growth" timber was finally depleted, the "hill hawks" looked elsewhere. Many went south, but a few found their way into the unspoiled Adirondacks.

———————————

The Rich Lumber Company rose and fell during the golden era of lumbering, during the days when it took more personal drive than capital expenditure to succeed in the lumber business. The Riches were to leave a perma-

nent mark on two of the three different states they operated in, not just the lingering railroad beds or old mill foundations, but also the thriving villages. It was thirty-three years of railroading through some of the northeast's finest virgin timber.

The company was founded by Herbert C. Rich and Horace Clarence Rich, first cousins from Cattaraugus, New York. Neither seems to have had any background in lumber manufacture, so it was apparently a case of opportunity breeding quick success. Herbert, who would soon become the dominant partner, established his first business venture in Gowanda, New York, where he opened up a hardware store, followed in time by a similar proprietorship in Cattaraugus.

In 1885, the partnership of cousins took root with their first venture at lumbering, a small operation at Clermont, Pennsylvania, the nature of which has been lost in history, but it was short-lived. The Riches by this time, however, had formed a hard working group that was to stay together for many years to come, despite the company migrations from one virgin timber stand to another.

In pioneer days it was an accepted practice to set up a

large but temporary sawmill to handle virgin cut, clean the area, and move on to another new cut with no intention of setting up a permanent facility or managing timberland on a sustained-yield basis. The Rich Lumber Company proved to be quite capable of creating a village when timber beckoned, and of dissolving a community when the land was bare. Railroads played an essential role in all they did.

With the successful completion of the first operation in Clermont, ambitions had been stirred and abilities unearthed. With a monetary stake supplied by a Mr. Burton, father-in-law of another first cousin, Odell Rich, Herbert C. and Horace Rich and company set out for another challenge to conquer.

Gardeau, Pennsylvania

The first Rich operation of any size was the venture at Gardeau, Pennsylvania, apparently successful despite a couple of setbacks when the sawmills burned. In 1886, Herbert C. and Horace moved into this hemlock-rich area and set up camp. The land, in the southeast corner of McKean County, was owned by a Col. Noel H. Parker and included what was to become the settlement of Gardeau, named after an Indian chief who once worked for Parker's father. The purchase of prime hemlock and hardwood timberlands was said to involve about seven thousand acres. A lease arrangement was made to use Parker's circular sawmill, at a rate of fifty cents per thousand board feet.

Parker's old mill soon burned to the ground. The Riches reached back to their home area in western New York and found two brothers, Royal B. and Heman R. Ford, capable of setting up their own large sawmill on location and sawing the Riches' timber on contract. So satisfactory was this marriage of talents that the arrangement was maintained on all operations throughout the entire lifespan of the Rich Lumber Company.

The Ford brothers used band mills, which were just becoming popular in large sawmills. This first mill built at Gardeau had the capability to saw better than 60,000 board feet of hemlock daily. It burned in October of 1893 and was rebuilt as a larger unit capable of turning out 75,000 board feet daily, and had a crew of fifty men. Two daily shifts of eleven hours each made a long workday, but the large backlog of timber melted fast into the whining band saws and this is what made money for the timber barons.

Fire again flattened the sawmill in March of 1897, a common hazard of this era. The mill was rebuilt once more, even though there was only about a year's supply of timber left in the Parker Run area.

Keystone Railroad

The limited methods of log transportation available in the late 1800s necessitated a logging railroad among the plateaus and adjoining steep lands of the Pennsylvania woods. The stream courses or runs had steep banks on either side, twisting for miles into timbered areas with, at times, hardly enough room for a creek bed at the bottom of the cut. Pennsylvania loggers were railroaders, and they pushed their tracks, or "tram," along about every named run or stream in the state, and also into many a run that never had a name.

Horses, in the past, had been effective, but it wasn't long before the Rich Lumber Company realized the need for a railroad to reach further so that they could feed their

The first locomotive owned by the Rich Lumber Company, next to a pile of hemlock logs near Gardeau, Pennsylvania. Shay No. 1 was a small 28-ton engine built in 1890. (*Collection of Thomas T. Taber III*)

urer; Herbert C. Rich, general manager; C. R. Rich and R. B. Ford, directors. The railroad was owned entirely by the Rich Lumber Company.

Motive power for the Gardeau railroad operations was provided by Shay locomotives, those popular geared engines with the three vertical cylinders on the right side of the boiler and the horizontal drive shaft along the right-hand outside face of the wheels. As a matter of fact, the Rich Lumber Company employed Shays exclusively on all four of their railroads, with one small exception in the New York operation. Five new Shays were purchased

hungry sawmills. In 1890, construction began on the tram, and rails were laid up Parker Run to reach the heart of the timber purchased from Noel Parker. In addition to Parker Run, the Riches had purchased all the land in Salt Works Run and in the area between Rock Run and Potato and North Creeks.

On April 23, 1891, the railroad was incorporated as the Keystone Railroad. Gardeau was on the Pennsylvania Railroad tracks, about three miles north of Sizerville, and the Keystone tracks ran northwesterly from there for about eight miles.

Officers of the Keystone Railroad were Horace C. Rich, president; W. F. Andrews, secretary; L. G. Willson, treas-

Contractor Claude Carlson, standing next to the handcar, transported his track-laying crew to their work location on this car which utilized a vertical pump bar. On the left is the Charles Abramson residence in Gardeau and on the right is the handcar storage building.

over the years, all of them from the Lima Locomotive Company in Lima, Ohio.

The first one purchased was a small 28-ton engine that arrived in 1890. It apparently was a little light for the job, having two trucks with only 28"-diameter wheels. Two more Shays arrived in 1894, one a 50- and the other a 35-ton.

With a good market for hemlock bark at the tanneries located throughout Pennsylvania, it was the custom to first fell the abundant hemlock and strip off the bark before cutting it into logs. The bark would be peeled off around the tree in four-foot segments and then piled in flat layers after drying. Hauled to the railroad siding with a horse and sled, it was then loaded onto flatcars for the journey to the tannery. As long as it was available, hemlock bark was found to be a relatively cheap source of tannin and tannic acid which was a principal ingredient of the leather tanning process. It acted upon animal skins to make them strong, flexible, and durable.

After removing the valuable bark, the logging crews would come through to cut the trees to proper log lengths and skid them to the rail siding. An early variety of the skeleton log car was then loaded with eight to twenty hemlock logs. In May of 1896, six of these cars, loaded with logs, burned in a fire along the railroad.

In 1898, the timber supply had been depleted in the area, and in March of that year sawmilling at Gardeau came to an end. The Riches, who actually spent little time in direct supervision of the lumber operations, had been busy acquiring new timberlands in another remote section of northwestern Pennsylvania. Within a few months after the sawing of the last log at Gardeau, the mill was dismantled, and along with the salvageable material from the buildings that once made up the settlement, it was loaded onto the railroad and sent to the next base of operations. With everything out, the rails were pulled up and the Keystone Railroad abandoned. The Riches were over at the other end of McKean County and waiting.

Granere, Pennsylvania

Preparations for the move of the Rich Lumber Company to Granere were actually started many months before the last log was sawn at Gardeau in 1898. The first purchase of standing timber had been made from the South Penn Oil Company in February of 1897 when 6,250 acres of old growth hemlock and hardwood timber were bought on the south branch of Kinzua Creek. The price was reported to be in the neighborhood of $150,000.

Construction of the new railroad and the new sawmill were begun in that same year in order to have the town in readiness when time came for the switchover. The three mill fires at Gardeau had convinced the Riches that metal was the best building material to use as far as the fire-prone sawmill was concerned.

The frame of the mill was constructed by the Berlin Iron Bridge Company of Berlin, Connecticut, and was covered by corrugated sheet metal. Cheaper insurance rates, it was hoped, would enable the mill to pay for itself in four years. As it turned out, the Granere sawmill operated only four years before timber depletion, but it never did burn.

This mill was even larger than the Gardeau mill, which was a single band mill capable of sawing 75,000 board feet in each eleven-hour shift. For about a year it ran on a two-shift basis, working around the clock to push 150,000 board feet of hemlock out the other end of the building every day. This was a capacity cut, however, and there were many shifts that couldn't exceed an average of 60,000 board feet per shift. The mill started production in 1898 and ran until 1901.

Rich Lumber Company believed in the best possible utilization (profit, in other words) of available species, and they contracted for a hardwood sawmill capable of producing 20,000 board feet per day. It was erected by Ventres and Company about a half-mile from Granere. A large shingle mill was also erected near the village. Hemlock bark was sent out by railroad, possibly to the large tannery at Mt. Jewett. Some seasons there would be as many as 12,000 cords of bark harvested.

The village of Granere was literally carved out of the woods to house the large working crew the Riches brought in for employment at the mill and in the woods. In time at least forty-five homes were built, plus a hotel, all of course owned by the Rich Lumber Company. The village had a population of about three hundred, plus as many as one hundred fifty workers in the woods as needed. Monthly payroll for the company ran from $10,000 to $12,000.

The company store, which sat next to the railroad tracks just below the sawmill, was actually the property of Rich Lumber and W. F. Andrews and was operated by Andrews. Homes were quite modest in construction, built entirely from local hemlock, and were susceptible to fire. At least one life is known to have been lost in a house fire during the brief existence of the village.

The office of Rich Lumber Company was also situated in Granere. L. G. Willson served as the superintendent of both the lumber company and railroad and was the right man for the job. Again the Riches stayed somewhat in the background using an able crew for field supervision.

In this part of the country, Swedes made up the bulk of the woods crews. They liked logging and worked hard.

Claude Carlson is remembered as an independent contractor who always had a hardworking bunch of contented Swedes. For many years Carlson contracted with Rich, taking on such chores as building the railroad right-of-ways and logging out the timber to the railroad sidings.

South Branch Railroad

The proposed new railroad was incorporated as the South Branch Railroad on May 7, 1897 and construction at Granere began that fall, the year before the big move from Gardeau. The length of trackage needed to connect the site of Granere with the nearest point on an existing railroad was soon constructed and in use.

There was a switch in officers' positions from the lineup of the old abandoned Keystone Railroad. Herbert C. Rich was now president, with Horace Rich stepping down to the vice presidency. Remaining as secretary was W. F. Andrews, but L. G. Willson was general manager as well as treasurer.

The outside terminal for the South Branch Railroad was in Mt. Jewett, a village located on or near many different railroad lines in the heart of McKean County on the Allegheny plateau of northwestern Pennsylvania. It was only about a four-mile trip down to Mt. Jewett from Granere, but the last 2.3 miles were over rented track rights. It was far more convenient to lease and use Elisha K. Kane's old logging line, later the Mead Run Railroad and part of the Mt. Jewett, Kinzua, and Riterville Railroad. The rental fee was $1,150 each year from 1898 to 1901 and after that date dropped to $500 annually.

Access was also obtained to the Erie Railroad in Mt. Jewett by leasing one hundred twenty-five feet of track rights from the Mt. Jewett, Kinzua, and Riterville Railroad in order for the South Branch Railroad to run its own

The village of Granere, Pennsylvania during the height of activity. Shay No. 3 is backing in toward the company store with the South Branch Railroad combine. Tracks on the right fan out among the sawmill lumber docks.

trains beyond the Mt. Jewett tannery to a point of connection with the Erie.

Granere was situated at the headwaters of the south branch of Kinzua Creek, and from this sawmill village the South Branch Railroad continued on in a westerly and northwesterly direction. The westerly terminal was known as Jury, near the spot where Hubert Run empties into the creek. The route could be located on the map as northwest of Lantz Corners, a small village on Route 6 in the Allegheny National Forest of northwest Pennsylvania. South Branch Junction, where Riches' own rail touched iron with the Mead Run Railroad, was about a mile north of Lantz Corners and on the west side of Route 219. Granere sat another mile or so into the woods in a westerly direction.

The total length of the South Branch Railroad was then

about eight miles. The number of short branches into the tributaries is unknown, but there probably were not many. As with the Keystone Railroad, all the locomotives used were the geared Shays. The company's original little Shay had been disposed of, but the other two Shays were brought up from Gardeau. One of these was eventually sold and replaced with a new 50-ton Shay in 1898.

Official rosters list the South Branch Railroad as having one passenger car and fifty-four freight cars, somewhat lopsided but indicative of its purpose. The published timetable shows that passengers had to take a backseat to logs and lumber. There was one late-afternoon train each day from Jury to Granere that laboriously pulled the single combination passenger car behind a string of log cars. It was a slow fifty-minute ride over that four miles.

On the other hand there were two daily trips (Sunday

excluded) from Granere on into Mt. Jewett, a somewhat faster thirty-minute jaunt over this other four-mile stretch. These ran in the early morning and at mid-day and consisted of cars loaded with sawn lumber, followed by a lonely combine. The return trip kept the town freshly supplied with goods from the outside world.

The fine hemlock cut soon came to an end, as all good timber usually managed to during that era. It was apparently less than four years before the axe and crosscut saw had all the hemlock dropped and the sawmill was left with no further log supply. The mill shut down in 1901. Granere was abandoned in 1902 and now had nothing to show except a few hunting camps.

As usual, the Riches were not idle in their exercising of foresight, and new timber tracts were purchased in a distant area, awaiting the rumble of the Shays after Granere was abandoned. This time, however, it was not to be the familiar hemlock that the company had been merchandizing so well for the last fourteen years. In fact, the operation was no longer to be on Pennsylvania soil.

Wanakena, New York

Cranberry Lake, located in the western portion of New York's Adirondack region, is a picturesque lake, long admired by sportsmen and camp-owners alike. Trout fishing at the turn of the century was superb, a treasured privilege for those able to gain access to this sparkling gem in the wilderness.

When Herbert C. Rich came into the area in 1901 to seek out and purchase land for the next home of his lumber domain, Cranberry Lake was still little-known. Cranberry Lake village, at the north end of the lake, had only about fifteen dwellings, and the lake was just beginning to be discovered by those with enough means to enjoy a summer home in the Adirondacks. The Carthage and Adirondack Railway had previously reached Oswegatchie station and Benson Mines in 1889, and in the early 1890s a road was cut through the woods from Newton Falls to Cranberry Lake village. This was the first direct link to the western Adirondacks. It would be the Rich Lumber Company, however, that really opened the door with the final railroad link, allowing the wealthy to ride right to the shore of the lake.

After the purchase of 16,000 acres of land and virgin timber on the southwest side of the lake in 1901, the Riches came back in 1902 ready to build a village, a task by then not difficult for them. The site was wisely chosen on Cranberry Lake itself, at the head of a long flow in the southwest corner where the Oswegatchie River entered the lake.

Actually the Riches were not the first to build at the location. Sternberg's Hotel, a sportsmen's camp, had been there for many years. It is said the Rich people stayed at the camp when first coming into the area. This camp was situated either on or near the old Albany Road, one of two old "military roads" that passed near Cranberry Lake. The Albany Road had been built in 1812, but eventually deteriorated because of disuse, reverting to a hunter's trail long before the Riches appeared.

Herbert C. Rich moved quickly. Soon a steam donkey engine was set up, at a point later to be the center of the village, and was kept busy uprooting tree stumps. The first building erected was the company store, soon followed by dwellings. Trainloads of hemlock lumber were brought in from Pennsylvania for house construction, much of it salvaged from homes dismantled at Granere.

Cranberry Lake was then still a wilderness retreat. The

Pine and spruce logs fringe the track newly laid through the Cranberry Lake wilderness.

Claude Carlson, right, and section crew display the tools used for railroad construction at Wanakena. From left to right: spiking hammer, shovel, tamping bar, railroad jack, grub hoe, and peavy. A rail gauge is on the ground behind Carlson.

gaunt tree stumps and driftwood in the flows created by the damming and raising of the lake in 1867 made a haven for wildlife and a home for large trout that would please anglers for many years to come. The rich green mantle of spruce and pine that dripped over the shoreline told the fortunate traveler that he need look no further. What are today bare rock ledges were once the shorelines and islands that harbored towering evergreens.

A small stream was dammed just above its mouth on the Oswegatchie River Flow and a sawmill was built, later to be followed by a variety of industrial mills. The sawmill was constructed and operated by the Ford brothers, and was an even larger double band mill.

It was probably 1903 before the sawmill got into full operation. A change in raw materials was in order; now spruce was the principal species to be sawn. However, lumber sizes and existing markets had changed but little from the hemlock days in Pennsylvania. A large amount of white pine was also sawn at Wanakena as well as what little hemlock that could be found.

Logging Railroad

Approximately fifteen miles of logging rails were built by the Riches, all within the township of Fine and, for the most part, south of the Wanakena site. The main branch, about ten miles in length, followed up Skate Creek and angled over to the Oswegatchie River which it followed as far as Boiling Springs, a short way below High Falls. This took the trains into the area known as "The Plains," a relatively level river plain rich with large white pine. Some of the logs were driven down this small river to a jackworks on the east bank where they could be taken out and loaded on the railroad cars.

Another two-mile branch worked its way southeasterly

An old growth white pine near the shore of Cranberry Lake is typical of the timber that was found in the region. (*Courtesy of Ted DeGroff*)

Shay No. 4 after its arrival at Wanakena. Conductor Bob Madison is standing in the center.

from the sawmill location to reach a jackworks at the head of Dead Creek Flow, a large backwater at the southwest extremity of Cranberry Lake. Logs were boomed down the lake to reach the sawmill via this short trip on rails. The only railroad logging north of Wanakena village was at Crimmins Switch, an access to a rail line laid around Cathedral Rock. There was also some logging activity along the Cranberry Lake Railroad, the common carrier line build by the Rich Lumber Company.

Original construction of the logging line is credited to John Olson for the most part, although Claude Carlson was active in building right-of-ways under contract. The abundance of Swedish names shows that the Riches brought most of their Pennsylvania crew with them to Wanakena and respected their hard work and capabilities. The logging railroad began operation about 1905.

Motive power on the logging pike was, as usual, the Shay locomotive exclusively. Shays No. 2 and 4, both 50 tons, were brought up from the Granere, Pennsylvania operation. In 1908, the boiler exploded on No. 2 while going up towards High Falls, at a spot just below Dobson's Trail. Apparently the water supply became dangerously low and the crown sheet burned through. At least one man was killed, a jewelry salesman who was along for the ride and was perched on one of the empty log cars in front of the locomotive. It is said that the brass number plate fell and struck him the fatal blow. Number 2 was rebuilt and renumbered as Shay No. 6. Gene Mattison was one of the more active locomotive engineers on the log trains.

Although the logging was all contracted, Rich Lumber Company used their own crews to load the railroad cars using the Barnhart steam loaders that sat on the log cars and moved along on top of them. Andy Rancier was one of the expert loader operators for the company, a skill

An outstanding sled-load of Adirondack white pine. The six logs, cut near Wanakena village, scaled 5,781 board feet.

11

The explosion of Shay No. 2 in 1908, on the High Falls branch, created bewilderment among the gathering bystanders who couldn't figure out how the engine crew survived. Railroad employee Hank Belcher is on the right.

which demanded practice but brought respect.

Locomotive and car repairs were done in the large machine shop which sat on the north side of the river at the edge of the village proper and west of the store. Several wooden tank cars, filled with water and loaded with several thousand feet of fire hose, could usually be seen on a siding near the machine shop. Forest fires presented a constant threat around sawmills and railroad activity, and it was that threat that the management was not allowed to forget. The year of 1908 is remembered as a year of terrible fires throughout the Adirondacks. A dry September and October created an abundance of extremely hazardous fuel in the form of logging slash left after the customary clear-cutting of pine and spruce.

Throughout the 16,000 acres of timberland there were about twelve logging camps built and run by the individual logging contractors, but coordinated by the Rich Lumber Company woods boss, Dick Hanley. Logs were usually moved to the railroad landings on two bunk sleds, though not the large two-sleds so common in the northeast. Pine cut along the edge of Cranberry Lake during the winter was sledded directly to the mill across the ice.

As was customary with most teamsters of this era, the care afforded the horses exceeded somewhat that given to the men. The teamster would literally tuck his team in at night, and in the morning would make the trip to the hovel to inspect their welfare his first duty. There's an old woods fable that the occasional snake now seen in the Adirondacks is there because of a few that were brought into the logging camps in bales of hay for logging horses.

Very little pulpwood was cut on the company property. It is reported that a trainload of spruce pulpwood was sent down to the mill at Newton Falls and plugged the mill so badly that little or none was sent down again.

The Barnhart log loader at work on "The Plains."

The Wanakena enginehouse on a cold morning with both Shays, Nos. 2 and 4, steaming up.

Industrial Complex

The Rich Lumber Company had profited from their full-utilization setup in Pennsylvania. At Wanakena an even greater variety of mills was established, all situated on the small millpond south of the Oswegatchie River. The pond was created by damming Skate Brook, and the mills were lined up along the north edge of the pond, all accessible to the logging railroad as it swung in from the southwest. In all cases the mills were constructed and operated by companies or individuals other than the Rich Lumber Company. This industrial complex allowed not only full-utilization of all species of timber, but also selection of logs for best use. Overall superintendent for the Rich Lumber Company was Leonard G. Willson, a kingpin in many of the company's endeavors.

Sawmill

Situated on the easterly end of the millpond was the large sawmill built by Royal and Heman Ford, sawing the lumber under contract for the Rich Lumber Company. This mill had two band saw headrigs, the longer carriage capable of sawing logs forty-eight feet long. Seldom were softwood logs taken into the mill that were less than twenty feet in length. Capacity production was about 75,000 board feet per day with good logs.

The claim has been made that this was one of the first sawmills to heat its log pond with steam in order to keep it open all winter; this was one of the coldest areas of the Adirondacks.

Andrew E. Race was sawmill manager for the Ford brothers and J. Otto Hamele, a man well-respected in com-

A panoramic view of the mill complex at Wanakena.

munity affairs, was millwright. Best known of the sawyers were Sid Bush on the long side and Gus Hegstrom on the smaller carriage.

At the east end of the sawmill were the usual long lumber docks, five of them, for the sorting and piling of lumber. Some of the docks were almost a half-mile long, which meant a long journey for the lumber as it was wheeled out by hand on one-axle dollies. Foreman on the docks was Charles Abramson, a job he held at all four sawmill towns created by the Rich Lumber Company.

The planing shed attached to the north side of the sawmill contained three planers: a four-sider, a one-sider, and a furring planer with ripsaw to make the much-in-demand 1 x 2's for plaster lath. Lumber was usually air-dried before planing. The foreman of this operation was a man named Burton.

A chip mill, operated by Pat Ryan and George Schlieder, was also associated with the sawmill. It was a unique operation which predated, by far, the modern development of chippers to utilize sawmill waste. It received the slabs and edgings from the sawmill, salvaged what lath could be made, and then rossed off the bark and chipped the waste material for sale to a pulp mill.

Whip Butt Mill

Next down the millpond, and behind the icehouse at pond's edge, was a mill to make turnings for the butt ends of buggy whips. Beech was used, apparently exclusively. The mill was said to be the largest of its kind in the world. Unfortunately the company went out of business in 1910.

The sawmill at Wanakena, owned and operated by the Ford brothers.

The heading mill manufactured barrelheads.

The shoe last factory was the last mill to operate at Wanakena.

The Setter Brothers' veneer mill at the western end of the mill complex is in the foreground. The branch from High Falls came in from the right.

Heading Mill

As one proceeded westerly along the pond, a large mill for the manufacture of barrelheads was located on the north side of a large storehouse. The mill could utilize any hardwood species and used a bolter saw to cut up the logs. Barrelheads were assembled and shipped out to various cooperage manufacturers.

Shoe Last Factory

Shoe lasts were turned out in the next mill which was owned by Charles Bates and run by Herbert Northrup. Lasts were wooden forms once used in shoe manufacture and repair, and were made exclusively from hard maple.

This mill burned on February 12, 1912, and was apparently the only mill in Wanakena to burn. The company's

Herbert C. Rich, on the right, poses with woods boss Dick Hanley on the left and Otto Hamele in the center.

fire record was definitely improving, but it was to be spoiled after the next move, which was to Vermont.

Veneer Mill

The Setter Brothers, a firm established in 1885 and based in the Riches' hometown of Cattaraugus, were persuaded by the Riches to build a veneer mill in Wanakena in 1902. Their business was to manufacture plywood and face stock for furniture. It was a long building at the far western end of the industrial complex. Ernest Horth, millwright with the company for fifty years, went to Wanakena to build the plant and remained there for the life of the mill.

The Wanakena mill operated only sporadically for nine years and used high-grade yellow birch exclusively. The better birch logs were not easy to come by at times because, reportedly, veneer logs were also brought into Wanakena by scow down the lake. Veneers cut on the rotary lathe in this relatively small mill were sent to Cattaraugus for further processing.

The Setters went on to build expanded operations in western New York and Ontario and were later absorbed by United States Plywood Corporation in 1963.

From this lineup of mills, it appears that almost every species of log could find a home if the logging crew found the tree that was profitable to cut and load on the railroad. Here was a marriage of markets that has seen very few equals since.

Cranberry Lake Railroad

The building of the wilderness sawmill village of Wanakena necessitated a connecting railroad at the turn of the century. In harmony with the Rich Lumber Company's experiences in Pennsylvania, construction of the village and manufacturing mills was planned around the

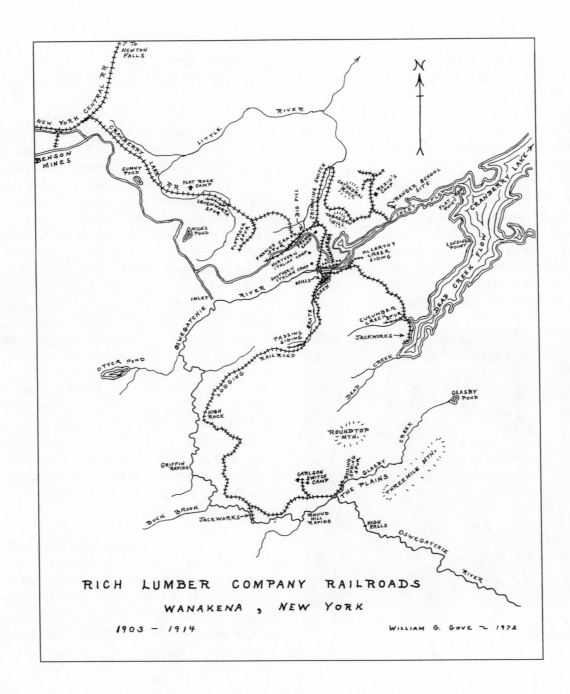

RICH LUMBER COMPANY RAILROADS

WANAKENA , NEW YORK

1903 - 1914

WILLIAM G. GOVE ~ 1972

18

concept of a common carrier line that would make a connection with a major railroad.

The Cranberry Lake Railroad was chartered on February 24, 1902, with the authority to lay rail from Benson Mines to Cranberry Lake. The building of the six-mile railroad was one of the first tasks undertaken in 1902, as clearing work began at the future site of Wanakena.

At the western terminal the connection was made, at Benson Mines, with the Carthage and Adirondack Railway, then being operated by the New York Central and Hudson River Railroad. The C&A Railway depot was used by the Cranberry Lake line. The official opening of the Cranberry Lake Railroad was on May 18, 1903.

Construction was with 60-pound, second-hand rail, laid on ties hewed on location from spruce, beech, birch, and maple logs. The main line had no span bridges, but did have an impressive 400-foot trestle constructed from round timbers. It was later filled in with iron ore sand and became known as the "big fill."

At the branch to the mill, across the Oswegatchie River, there was an attractive "pony lattice" bridge on concrete masonry. The total cost of road and equipment was almost $82,000.

Motive power for the first two years was the two Shay locomotives, Nos. 2 and 4, that also served the logging line. In 1905, a new "rod" or conventional-type locomotive was purchased from the Lima Locomotive Company to take over the chores on the passenger line and relieve the Shays. It was a 51-ton Consolidation-type 2-8-0 and cost about $9,000 at the time. This able little Lima effectively handled the duties of moving the coach and combine plus the shipments of lumber and various freight items. Other rolling stock, bedsides the two passenger cars, was listed as being twenty flatcars and twenty-seven log cars, all

The "big fill" trestle on the Cranberry Lake Railroad main line in 1908.

equipped with automatic couplers and air brakes. All three of the locomotives were lettered "Cranberry Lake Railroad." Small gasoline-powered cars, or speeders, were used, at times, for small payload runs.

Earnings of the railroad corporation were quite favorable, something not always true of a captive railroad serving a lumber company. After surviving a deficit in the fledgling year of 1903, net earnings fluctuated between $3,000 and $5,000 annually. The fact that between eighteen and twenty-one thousand passengers were carried each

The small Lima rod engine used on the Cranberry Lake Railroad at Wanakena village.

The Cranberry Lake Railroad junctioned with the New York Central and Hudson River Railroad at Benson Mines.

year shows that it was not only the little village of Wanakena that was being served; a new access had been opened up for summer vacationers who had established camps on Cranberry Lake. Lumber and other forest products were the major freight commodities to move to Benson Mines with a much smaller return tonnage of flour, grain, meat, and other provisions, in all totaling better than 50,000 tons per year.

Forest products of other mill operations also found their way to the Cranberry Lake Railroad since this was really the only convenient way out of the woods, except going down the lower Oswegatchie River.

The John McDonald Lumber Company had a rossing mill on Barber's Point on the lake to ross, or debark, and slash softwood. They sent the wood and hemlock bark by scow to Wanakena for railroad shipment, until their plant was destroyed by the big fires of 1908. Dana and Brahm Bissell had a small sawmill at Cranberry Lake village and shipped lumber on a barge behind the boat, *Merrimac*, to Wanakena for loading onto railroad boxcars. This, of course, predated by many years the large sawmill and railroad line from the east that Emporium Forestry Company was to give Cranberry Lake village.

The new list of railroad corporation officers, slightly different from the previous South Branch Railroad, was as follows: Herbert C. Rich, president; Horace Clarence Rich, vice president; Clayton R. Rich, secretary; Leonard G. Willson, treasurer and supervisor; and E. E. Keith, auditor.

Speeders were used on the Cranberry Lake line.

There were fifteen stockholders with par value of stock listed at $80,000.

There were about twenty-seven employees in all, including officials. This included a track force of eleven which may have been kept quite busy after the 1904 visit of a New York State Railroad Commission inspector who reported that the grading was deficient and the cuts poorly ditched. The regular engineer of the train was Eugene Blodgett with Chub Mattison as conductor.

Though only six miles long, the line was, at times, graced with dignitaries. The elegant private railroad car of New York Central president, Chauncey M. Depew, was occasionally seen parked on the dock spur at Wanakena.

Camps According to Nationality

At one time there were as many as 1,500 people getting their mail through the Wanakena post office. Not that they were all living at Wanakena village—many were in the various camps of different types. Noteworthy is the contrast with modern accepted standards, because at Wanakena each nationality had it own camp; there was little mingling.

The loggers' camps usually were located on the railroad and were primarily manned by Swedes and Italians. As camps were remote and inaccessible, lumberjack minister Charles Atwood found logging railroads to be the most practical way of traveling to the various camps he wanted to preach at in the Adirondacks, whether using a powered speeder on loan from a lumber company or peddling his bicycle over the many long miles.

Logging camps often had their problems with certain uninvited guests such as bedbugs and lice, but lumberjacks had ways of dealing with these pests. If good strong yellow soap didn't get them, it might mean getting out the copper kettle and boiling the clothes and straw mattress coverings, to be filled afterward with fresh straw from the barn. A good spray of kerosene on the bunk boards would discourage the pesky bedbugs for about two weeks and give the logger a few itch-free nights.

Drinking was not permitted in most of the logging camps, but an exception was made in the case of the Italian camps as alcohol had always been an essential element of their homeland diet, and the Italian laborers wouldn't work without it. In view of their hard work, the exception was a wise compromise. The crew of the log train was startled one day, in 1906, while going out the Dead Creek Flow branch. As they were about to pass the logging camp of jobber Joe Rezio, on the east side of the track about a mile before the flow, Joe came running out to stop the train, waving and jumping for joy at the birth of his son, Daley, that morning. This was sufficient cause for a drink for all in the train crew.

A larger camp of Italian workers was established in the woods just west of Wanakena village. As usual it was necessary to separate the immigrants from northern and southern Italy, bitter enemies who sometimes didn't hesitate to settle an argument with a knife. This camp supplied workers for the various mills at Wanakena; hardworking Italians who saved their money and often returned to Italy to finish their years. To economize they maintained a skimpy diet—dark bread and cheese.

Although drinking was allowed in their camp, it was strictly forbidden for the Italians to sell liquor. On one occasion a group from the northern Italian camp was caught selling liquor and ordered to appear in court at the county seat of Fine. While traveling the early morning train to the village of Fine on the day of the court appearance, the group consumed a considerable quantity of alcohol, and in their jovial condition hatched a scheme to beat "John Law." Only one of the Italians pleaded guilty and all the witnesses stated they had bought the liquor from that one person. On the way home the gang all chipped in to pay the person's fine and nobody was out very much. Needless to say, the spirits continued to flow.

The French workers' camp was located on the railroad about two miles from Wanakena toward Benson Mines. The site is near the present Route 3 and is now covered by a pine plantation.

Wanakena Village

Many of the inhabitants of Wanakena who came with the Rich Lumber Company from Pennsylvania were Swedes. Fine little homes were built for them by the company, in contrast to the cruder woods camps, and many of these houses still stand today.

The village got its name back in 1902 while being built. Herbert C. Rich recalled that he had seen the name "Wanakena" on a streetcar in Buffalo and, liking the sound of the name, chose it for his new village. At its peak, Wanakena village had a railroad depot, a restaurant, two hotels, a boarding home, a large general store, and a clubhouse with library, reading room, and bowling alley.

The large general store was owned and operated by Clayton Rich, brother of Herbert C. Rich, and Wally F. Andrews, the same pair that had operated the store at

Granere. A railroad siding along the back of the store was used for unloading store supplies and ice into the icehouse next door. It was here, also, that the Rich and Andrews' store would load railroad flatcars with supplies for the log camps. Orders such as fifty bushels of potatoes or one hundred pounds of coffee, which first had to be hand ground at the store, were typical. A nephew of Clayton Rich, Herbert Rich (not Herbert C.), recalls working at the store, but since he had to live in an unheated, top-floor hotel room with outside temperatures occasionally reaching –40°, he stayed only one winter.

The boarding house was operated by the Conroy family and housed the workers who wouldn't think of staying at the Italian or French camps. Another nephew of Herbert C. Rich, Claude Rich, was, at first, manager of the express office among other duties, but was in time to take on greater responsibilities as the original Riches grew older.

Wanakena became quite a busy location during the summer months with vacationers and camp residents. Steam-powered passenger boats navigated the West Inlet Flow up to the Wanakena dock, except during the dry summer period of late August when the water was low. There was a daily excursion around the lake by one of these boats, stopping at all the hotel and cottage docks along the lake for passengers, freight, and mail, and reaching Wanakena by noon to connect with the train leaving for Benson Mines. Afterwards it would return to the home dock at Cranberry Lake village. It was usually the steamboat, *Helen*, but the Rich Lumber Company also owned a gasoline-powered passenger launch, the *Wanakena*. The company later sold the *Wanakena* and a smaller racing boat, the *Comet*, to the Holland brothers, owners of the *Helen*. It is said that the popular *Helen* sank at least once a year, one of the numerous floating logs ramming through her hull.

The depot at Wanakena sat beyond the store. The track down to the boat landing is in the background. The post office was in a house on the left.

The arrival of the morning train from Benson Mines presented a busy scene.

Bissell's railroad loading dock on the flow at Wanakena. Note the barge in the foreground on which the lumber was towed up the lake from the sawmill site at Cranberry Lake village.

The Exodus from Wanakena

The Adirondack timber purchase lasted longer than the company's Pennsylvania operations, but within a little less than eight years the virgin timber growth was about gone. What the logger hadn't stripped off, the terrible fires of that era had. The sawmill was shut down in 1910; no more of the fine spruce or pine sawlogs were left. Some of the smaller mills continued operating on what little hardwood was left, the heading mill being the last to shut down in 1912.

Again, the Rich Lumber Company planned the purchase of another timber tract that they could move the en-tire operation to, and by the time the last of the Wanakena mills shut down, a site had been selected in Vermont that was ripe for a sawmill and village. But Wanakena did not die a sudden death as had its two previous Pennsylvanian counterparts. Summer camp life on Cranberry Lake was at the height of popularity, and the Riches' Cranberry Lake Railroad was still quite active.

The homes were gradually sold to their occupants and camp lots along the inlet were laid out with seventy-five feet of frontage. The price was fifty dollars a lot on the north side of the river and twenty-five dollars on the south side. The store was sold to businessman J. Otto

The steamboat, *Helen*, on the left, was a familiar sight on Cranberry Lake. The Rich Lumber Company's motor launch, *Wanakena*, is on the right.

Hamele, who operated it successfully for many years.

However, Wanakena village did not retain its prominence for long as the primary link between Cranberry Lake and the outside world. The Emporium Forestry Company, another Pennsylvania concern looking for virgin territory to conquer, had set up a new sawmill village at Conifer, sixteen miles east of Cranberry Lake village in 1911. In 1913, the year after the Rich Lumber Company moved to Vermont, the Emporium Forestry Company pushed its Grasse River Railroad through to Cranberry Lake village, and another link to the big cities was created, connecting with the New York Central Adirondack Division at Childwold. This proved to be a more practical and enduring rail access than the Rich Lumber Company-owned common carrier line running west. The Cranberry Lake Railroad operated one more year before ceasing operations, and the assets were sold at a receiver's sale on September 1, 1914, followed shortly thereafter by dissolution of the corporation. The rails were pulled up by 1917.

The 16,000 acres of timberland were, by now, a desolate area of logging slash and gaunt tree skeletons left by forest fires, and disposal of the land was a matter of concern. An idea was born in the mind of J. Otto Hamele of the Rich Lumber Company that the cutover lands could serve a

Huge pine stumps from the Rich Lumber Company cuttings linger amidst the growth of new softwood trees. (*Photo by Bill Gove*)

useful purpose if used as an experimental area for forestry students. From his suggestion the New York State Ranger School at Wanakena, the oldest school of its kind in North America, was created. The Rich Lumber Company donated a 1,814-acre forest tract on the West Inlet Flow to the State University College of Forestry in Syracuse, and in the fall of 1912 the first students arrived by railroad, having as their first task the clearing of the site two miles east of Wanakena village and the erecting of the first buildings.

The remainder of the Rich Lumber Company timber-lands was sold to the state of New York and incorporated into the Adirondack Forest Preserve. A new growth of pine and spruce is evident along the plains now, growing amidst the huge pine stumps from the Rich Lumber Company days. A new growth of hardwood trees blankets the ridges, living testimony to the renewable character of timber resources.

The exodus of the Rich Lumber Company was not the end of sawmill activity on Cranberry Lake. The Emporium Lumber Company built a large band mill at Cranberry Lake village in 1917, which operated for ten years.

Manchester, Vermont

The move of the Rich Lumber Company to Vermont was to be the final transfer the corporation would make. Harvesting of timber had been exhausted on their land in the Adirondacks, profits had been pocketed, and ambitions were still rife. As matters turned out, experience gained from three major sawmill village creations did not stand them in the best stead. Manchester might possibly have been the company's Waterloo had it not been for the advent of the First World War.

The picturesque little village of Manchester, Vermont was once the scene of three busy railroads, all active in a commercial activity that differed considerably from the recreation-oriented economy that changed the face of this quiet community on the western side of the Green Mountains. In addition to being situated on the Rutland Railroad, eventually the Vermont Railway, Manchester also served as the terminal of the five-mile-long Manchester, Dorset, and Granville Railroad, a line that, from 1904 to 1918, conveyed passengers and marble.

Marble quarrying activities in the area were still at their height when Herbert Rich went to Manchester in 1912, investigating what had been reported to be a promising cut of Green Mountain spruce. Within two years the Riches gave Manchester its third railroad, carved indelibly into the side of East Mountain.

During 1912, negotiations were completed for the purchase of standing timber on a 12,000-acre tract, buying the stumpage only. Arrangements were made through the First National Bank of Boston. From the assumed cruise figures, it was estimated that the mill would have a fifteen-year working life, and plans went forward on this presumption. A 116-acre farm was purchased from Frank Walker on the East Manchester Road for a site on which to build the sawmill and the customary company homes. Late in 1912, a railroad siding was built to the proposed mill site from the nearby Rutland Railroad.

The Vermont operation, incorporated for $200,000, was comprised of Herbert C. Rich, president; Leonard G. Willson, vice president; and Claude A. Rich, treasurer and general manager. Claude moved to Manchester and became quite active in the direct management of the company. He was the thirty-two-year-old nephew of Herbert C. Rich, and was considered to be a nice person to work for. Herbert carried on his administrative duties from his residence in Cattaraugus, New York. Erie Eddy Rich, an adopted son of Herbert C., also became active in the Manchester operation.

Construction of the double band sawmill began in 1912 at a site on the former Walker farm where Lye Brook flows west through a gorge from the top of the East Mountain plateau. The sawmill was similar to that built at Wanakena, using two carriages capable of sawing 70,000 board feet in the customary ten-hour day, but averaging about 55,000 feet. As usual, the sawmill was owned and operated by the Ford brothers, sawing under contract for the Rich Lumber Company and using machinery transferred to Manchester when the Wanakena mill was dismantled. The mill operated fifty weeks per year, six full days a week, producing about sixteen million board feet of spruce lumber annually.

The industrial complex of Wanakena was not duplicated here at Manchester, but Patrick J. Ryan and George R. Schlieder did set up their chip plant again on the north side of the sawmill. After salvaging what lath could be made from the slabs and edging, all waste wood was rossed of bark and fed through a chipper. The wood chips

Sawmill at Manchester, Vermont, built by the Ford brothers. The chipping plant of Ryan and Schlieder is to the left.

Neat stacks of spruce lumber conceal most of the sawmill as a Rutland Railroad flat is ready to roll with its consignment of spruce dimension and lath.

were sent to a sulphite pulp mill at Malone, New York. This resulted in the heralded development of a pulpwood chip industry that utilized wood waste based on the same basic techniques long ago practiced by the Rich Lumber Company.

In the waste that was considered unsuitable for anything but the teepee burner, there was still one more use. Kindling wood was pulled from the conveyor trough by workers who were paid seventy-five cents per cord to pick it out, tie it in bundles, and pile it. This was shipped out by rail to the metropolitan areas.

The general store, built on the east side of the town highway, along with a group of houses built on a knoll just to the south, again came under the proprietorship of

Rich and Andrews. These homes were owned and maintained by Rich and Andrews for their employees, while the company officers owned their own homes on the west side of the highway. The years 1913 and 1914 were a busy time of building on this once quiet meadowland south of Manchester Depot. Many preparations were in order to begin turning the wheels of a new industry that would support a labor force varying from two hundred fifty to four hundred, depending on the season.

On July 5, 1914, the sawmill began full-scale production and spruce lumber soon filled the sticking yard. Hopes were high for many prosperous years ahead. After all—hadn't the reports promised enough timber to last for at least fifteen more years?

The steep portion of the logging railroad can be traced in this view overlooking the sawmill and settlement. The railroad followed Lye Brook which angled upwards from the left to the top center to put the rails on top of the plateau. Rutland RR main line is in the foreground.

Shay No. 6 holding back a heavy load as the train approaches the upper switch on the switchback in 1916.

Logging Railroad

To climb the rugged western edge of the Green Mountain range is a hard enough task on foot, but the prospect of building a standard gauge railroad up the steep slope would be a task for only the courageous of heart. To reach their timber resource the Rich Lumber Company had to not only climb the mountain with their railroad, but also keep it at a grade that would be feasible to negotiate with a loaded train. Here they had to surmount grades never before experienced on previous operations. And they did. But here they did not have to contend with the movement of passengers and freight into the sawmill village and

thus, for the first time, had no common carrier charter.

Work crews of Italian immigrants literally carved out the railroad's right-of-way out of the side of East Mountain to reach the extensive plateau. As Leonard G. Willson himself surveyed the route, he found there was no choice but to follow the course of Lye Brook where it cut down through a hollow to tumble off the Green Mountain range. Even here the grade was excessive and necessitated a switchback about two and one-half miles up from the mill. A switchback is a simple scheme of building a zigzag or dogleg back up the hill to gain elevation at the sacrifice of forward progress. Maximum grade was thus kept

29

Shay No. 6 crossing the "high trestle" with a full trainload.

down to about six percent, acceptable for a Shay locomotive but putting restraint on operational procedures.

Duncan Stewart, of Salamanca, New York, built the many trestles and bridges under contract, another task far more formidable than experienced on the other three railroads built by the company. The picturesque "high trestle" towered about sixty-five feet over the foot of a narrow ravine.

Once on the top of the Green Mountain range, the secondhand, 60-pound rail was laid beyond the headwaters of Lye Brook in Sunderland township and northeasterly around Bourn Pond into Winhall Township and the Bourn Brook drainage. The railroad ended at the headwaters of the Winhall River — in all, sixteen miles of roadbed, including spurs. The first delivery of logs was made to the completed and waiting sawmill in April 1914.

As was now the customary practice for the Rich Lumber Company, two locomotives were used to handle the logging chores, both Shays. Shay No. 6 was brought with the company from Wanakena, and was joined in that first operational year by another brand new Shay, one of almost equal weight (fifty tons), but having only two-wheel trucks instead of three. The new engine was tagged "No. 7" and was the last locomotive the company was to buy. The other engines used at Wanakena had been disposed of by that time.

Other railroad equipment brought from Wanakena included ten flatcars, twenty-four logging cars, a log loader, and a snowplow — all equipped with air brakes. The Vermont terrain made demands on an adequate braking system. Although the snowplow had a very practical seasonal use, it is doubtful that the log loader saw much service. The company had previously used Barnhart loaders, but apparently at Manchester the logs were all loaded by

Spotting empties into Joe Rizio's landing near the top of the steep Lye Brook grade.

Landing at Diot's camp on the Winhall River, near the end of the logging railroad.

hand from high skidways using company crews.

The well-equipped engine shop was located just north of the sawmill, and operated under the direction of Henry Schoolmaster who came from the Erie Railroad shop at Bradford, Pennsylvania.

On the regular crew with Shay No. 6 was Johnny Tinder as engineer and fireman Bill House. Normally assigned to Shay No. 7 was Gene Mattison, engineer; Archie Eaton, fireman; Leslie N. Jacklin, brakeman; and Alva Belcher, conductor. Most of these men had formerly worked on larger railroads in western New York, the Riches' home territory, and stuck faithfully with the company in their migrations.

The regular operating procedure when using both loco-motives was for No. 6 engine to go up the mountain early in the morning and to spend the day shifting cars to be loaded at the various sidings. Shay No. 7 would make two round trips per day on of the mountain, bringing down nine loaded cars on each trip. Since the Shay could push only seven empty cars up the steep mountain grade, it would necessitate an occasional extra trip up with empty cars. The engine would back up the mountain, pushing the empties in front of it. If there were any more loaded cars left at the end of the afternoon, Shay No. 6 would bring them down when returning home.

The train crew normally worked from 7 A.M. to 5 P.M. and would be responsible for unloading the log cars at the millpond dumping ramp. The night watchman had the

Topping off a car with small spruce logs at Rizio's landing on Lye Brook meadow in 1914. Tom Smith is on the right.

duty of loading the tenders with coal each night.

The only known accident occurred in the third month that the railroad was operating. The locomotive was usually run at the head end while going downhill with a heavy load, but on the middle leg of the switchback the order would be reversed, and the log cars would have nothing to stop them if they broke loose. On June 19, 1914, a loaded car got away and went careening down the mountain with crewmen John Marone and Mark Yalgel aboard. The injuries they received when jumping off led to a $40,000 lawsuit against the company.

From that date on it was a company order that all of the train crew would ride in the locomotive while descending the switchback and that the brakes be set at the upper switch. Archie Eaton recalled an occasion when the sand-pipe on the locomotive became plugged and the train slid down the snow-covered rails on the switchback at an alarming rate of speed. He was crouched and ready to jump, but there was an uphill pitch on the track beyond the switch that brought the heavy load to a safe stop.

There was a safety spur in the mill yard just before reaching the log dump, with the switch always kept lined in preparation for other runaways. However, there apparently were no other incidents or accidents other than occasional derailments.

Fireman Archie Eaton decided that he would combine some bear trapping on the mountains with his daily trips. Three bear traps were put out with a large codfish hanging over the center of each, and flags were set to go up when the traps were sprung. The flags were visible from the locomotive as it made its way up the hill. Only once did Archie spot a raised flag; they stopped the train on the way back down that afternoon. Sure enough there was a bear, and conductor Hank Belcher begged for the privilege of killing it with the axe. He soon came trotting back to the train—too scared to perform the deed. Archie then dispatched the bear with his axe.

On occasions when the crew wasn't rushed, the blueberry fields on the plateau received their attention. The large areas of previous burns were rich with berries.

Logging camps were operated by the various logging contractors who had taken on the job of cutting and putting the logs railside. Just the spruce and fir were cut, and judging by photographs of the operation, the size and quality left a lot to be desired. Certainly the logs were not of the size the company had been accustomed to in the past.

About mid-1919 reports began to filter down that the timber appeared to be running out. By fall the rumors were confirmed. But how could this be? Had not the pur-

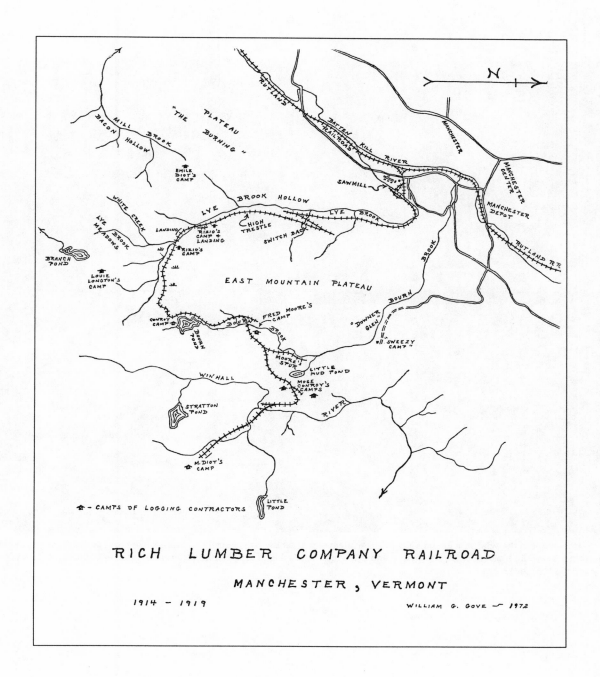

RICH LUMBER COMPANY RAILROAD

MANCHESTER, VERMONT

1914 – 1919   WILLIAM G. GOVE — 1972

Engineer Gene Mattison opens the whistle wide on Shay No. 6 while perched on the "high trestle." The crew, backing up the mountain with seven empty cars, also includes fireman Bill House in the cab doorway and brakemen Les Jackland and Hank Belcher on the tail end. Note the heavy wood beams on the skeleton log cars and the air brakes.

Unload at the millpond log dump. The train crew of Shay No. 7 has released the chains and is working the logs off of the tilted cars.

A load of seven cars of spruce easing down the switchback provides a scenic picture overlooking the Manchester valley. The crew all rode in the locomotive cab during this leg of the journey.

chase figures indicated a fifteen-year operating life? And here the operation had only been in progress five and one-half years.

Someone had either made an error in grossly miscalculating the standing timber volume or had been the victim of a large-scale misrepresentation. There is a report that the 12,000 acres turned out to be 7,500. At any rate, the timber was gone. The Rich Lumber Company would have taken a large financial loss on this operation had it not been for the war. World War I broke out the same year that the Manchester sawmill began, boosting prices enough to overcome what would have been a disastrous loss because of a meager timber supply.

The company had maintained a good fire record for the last few years, but Manchester was to finish up operations by spoiling this. On June 18, 1918, a fire started in a hot box in the Ryan and Schlieder chip plant which did $20,000 worth of damage to that part of the mill. Insurance covered $6,000 of this, and it was rebuilt.

Then just two weeks before the mill was rumored to be shutting down because of timber depletion, a blow intervened that resolved any indecision. At two o'clock on the afternoon of October 29, 1919, a fire started in the sawmill that soon reduced to ashes an industry still supporting a work force exceeding three hundred. Seventy-four-year-old laborer, Cary Reynolds, who worked on the slasher saw in the mill, ran back in to grab his lunch pail and was never seen again. The $50,000 loss was only half-covered by insurance; there didn't appear to be any suspicion of foul play in connection with the fire.

Thus the Rich Lumber Company came to an inglorious end on the outskirts of this picturesque Vermont village. Herbert C. Rich had apparently lost his zeal to seek out new hills of towering evergreens over which to lay rails. The company was liquidated in 1920, closing out thirty-four years of successful operations in three states.

This wasn't quite the end of sawmilling for the Rich interests, however. Some of the Rich Lumber Company stockholders decided to make yet another attempt to harvest Vermont timber. There was still hardwood left on their cutover lands as well as other plentiful supplies of maple and birch logs that could be trucked to the Manchester location.

In 1920, the N. D. Cass Company was formed, joining the forces of Walter F. Andrews, Patrick J. Ryan, George R. Schlieder, and Claude A. Rich, with toymaker Nathan D. Cass of Massachusetts. By this time Herbert C. Rich was in retirement in western New York, but nephew Claude Rich had made a permanent home in Vermont.

The former Rich sawmill site was purchased and a sawmill and toy factory built in 1920. A 5,133-acre land purchase from the Bourn Cooperage Company assured them of a future hardwood timber supply. However, it was fire again that brought a finish to the sawmill which burned completely in 1925. There was never again any sawmilling undertaken by any of the Rich family. The Vermont timberlands that fed their whining band mills are now part of the Green Mountain National Forest. Manchester was to have more sawmills in the future but never again any the size of the large band mills.

Only the settlement of Richville remained, retaining most of the homes built by the company in 1912 and 1913. As with the lingering village of Wanakena, it was a quiet settlement, providing rural homes for many descendants of the hardworking families that came to town with the Rich Lumber Company, a progressive leader of its era.

Locomotive Roster — Rich Lumber Company Operations

Keystone Railroad — Gardeau, Pa., 1889-1897

Number	Type	Builder	Bldr. No.	Trucks	Cyl. & Drivers	Weight	Built	Source	Disposition
1	Shay	Lima	309	2	9" x 8" — 28"	28	8/1890	New	Chehalis Riv. Lbr. Co. Chehalis, Wash.
2	Shay	Lima	464	3	12" x 12" — 32"	50	3/1894	New	
3	Shay	Lima	465	2	10" x 10" — 29"	35	6/1894	New	

South Branch Railroad — Granere, Pa., 1897-1902

Number	Type	Builder	Bldr. No.	Trucks	Cyl. & Drivers	Weight	Built	Source	Disposition
2	Shay	Lima	464						
3	Shay	Lima	465						Lake Erie, Franklin & Clarion RR, Clarion, Pa.
4	Shay	Lima	553	3	12" x 12" — 32"	50	4/1898	New	

Rich Lumber Company Railroad & Cranberry Lake Railroad — Wanakena, N.Y., 1902-1914

Number	Type	Builder	Bldr. No.	Trucks	Cyl. & Drivers	Weight	Built	Source	Disposition
2	Shay	Lima	464						Exploded 1908, rebuilt as No. 6 1914 – Basic Refractories Co. Natural Bridge, N.Y.
4	Shay	Lima	553						
5	2-8-0	Lima	1015		17" x 20" — 40"	51	1905	New	

Rich Lumber Company Company — Manchester, Vt., 1914-1919

Number	Type	Builder	Bldr. No.	Trucks	Cyl. & Drivers	Weight	Built	Source	Disposition
6	Shay	Lima	464	3	12" x 12" — 32"	50		Former No. 2	1919 – Jackman Lbr. Co., Jackman, Me., became No. 1
7	Shay	Lima	2746	2	11" x 12" — 32"	50	1914	New	1919 – E.E. Jackson ____ Co., Riderwood, Ala.

2

The Emporium Lumber Company

by William Gove

Pennsylvania Operation

If ever there was a king of railroad logging in the northeast, it would have been William L. Sykes. For sixty-seven years Sykes and his Emporium Lumber Company reigned supreme. For two generations they stood alongside their brethren in the softwood fraternity. The story of Sykes is one of initiative, drive, and resourcefulness—one that could never be repeated today and thus is relegated to the colorful history of the lumber industry. William L. Sykes was born in 1859 at Round Island, Pennsylvania, near Williamsport. This was at the time when Pennsylvania was leading the entire nation in lumber production. The giant pine and hemlock lorded supreme in the Allegheny hills.

Brought up by a father who was a skilled woodturner, his early training developed a personality not only rich in kindness and religious devotion, but also one of absolute independence. In later years he built a meeting hall for his Methodist Church in the solid Roman Catholic community of St. Mary's, despite the threat that he would be run out of town if he attempted it.

This spirit of independence, coupled with an inventive drive, soon led him on the path of building a hardwood lumber domain second to none. The beginning was insignificant—a small mill at Howard Siding and possibly one or two others in the Benzinger area. This soon sharpened his hunger for more wood.

His first mill of any consequence was in the little Elk County community of Benzinger, five miles east of St. Mary's. The year was 1882 and Sykes realized that additional capital would be needed if he was to continue to grow, and he knew how to seek out and convince associates who could provide it.

The following year a new partner, William S. Caflisch, was taken in, along with his investment of $6,000, and the firm of Sykes and Caflisch was formed. Now Sykes' drive and initiative were combined with the all-consuming drive of that new partner.

Caflisch became the number two stockholder. This energetic but impulsive immigrant from the Alsace-Lorraine region of Germany was to become a valuable partner for many years, and before long, W. L. Sykes' brother-in-law.

The Benzinger, Pennsylvania sawmill about 1900. The logging line comes in from the left; the boxcars are setting on a railroad siding. Note the clear cutting right to the edge of the village.

Early Pennsylvania Logging

The topography of the Pennsylvania hills was such that many unique logging schemes were devised out of necessity. The ravines, or "runs" as they were called in Pennsylvania, were often deep and the banks steep on both sides, with just about enough space in the bottom of the run for the creek bed. The plateaus on top were rich in timber growth, but it was down the runs that the logs had to be conveyed. The earliest loggers had direct access to the large rivers for rafting of the logs, but the "hill hawks" soon found themselves walking the narrow runs.

Log slides were built down the steep slopes and were constructed of two lines of logs laid tightly together, each hewn on the face to make a trough. Gravity supplied the force, helped by some grease or ice if necessary. Care was taken not to put a small log between two large ones, or it would be pounded to splinters before reaching is destination, and care was taken by the men working at the landing who had a deep respect for the logs speeding downhill. The landing was characterized by the broken stubs of what were once trees of all sizes before being hit by the logs flying down the slide.

The log trails or slides were also built on the levels or down the gentler hollows, and horses would pull trains of logs along the slides. This was a scheme which, in an improved form, was later to be introduced into the Adirondacks and gave New Yorkers something to talk about.

If the slope wasn't too severe, a horse might be seen

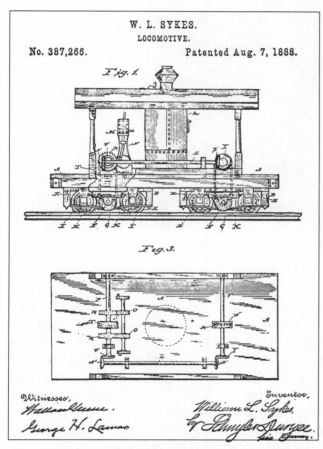

W. L. Sykes' first locomotive, the old "Barney," on a log job near Benzinger in 1882 with a few youngsters and women along for the ride. A planked horse road can be seen in the foreground.

The original patent drawing for old "Barney," which was built in 1882.

"Barney" had all four axles powered by a chain and sprocket drive and only weighed eight tons.

41

Old "Barney" with a trainload of logs ready for unloading into the log pond at the Benzinger sawmill about 1896. W. T. Turner is the man with the straw hat and scale stick. Note the fine cherry logs in the foreground and the spring poles used to tighten the chains on the log cars.

pulling a long train of logs down the hill on bare earth without a slide. Many logs would be joined end to end with grapple hooks.

These were the schemes used by Sykes and Caflisch as they logged Elk County in the upper part of West Creek, Bear Run, and Little Bear. As was the custom, huge piles of logs would be accumulated at landings along the run. From that point there was only one answer for transporting the logs to the sawmill, a railroad.

Sykes was frequently heard to repeat the oft-quoted "necessity is the mother of invention." At Benzinger he built a three-foot-gauge railroad over a distance of about three miles back into the woods and relaid several locations. Using only 16-pound rail, he couldn't buy a locomo-

tive light enough for the job so he decreed he would make his own, not too big of a project for his inventive mind.

In 1885, Sykes built old "Barney." There wasn't much to Barney. Essentially it was a short platform supported on two trucks, with an upright boiler in the center and a pair of steam engines on the front end. All four axles were powered by means of a longitudinal shaft on the platform, bevel gears, and a chain sprocket drive. The locomotive weighed only eight tons with coal and water.

Old Barney was used about Benzinger until it was sold, in 1897, to John DuBois and was last used on a Hicks Run logging railroad around 1900. Barney was only the first of many locomotives to come under Sykes' wing.

Another homemade geared locomotive was constructed

The Emporium Lumber Company sawmill at Keating Summit, Pennsylvania, after it was rebuilt following the 1901 fire. The Pennsylvania Railroad main line is in the left background. (*Collection of Thomas T. Taber III*)

in 1887 at the Struthers Wells and Company shop in Warren, Pennsylvania for the express purpose of leasing it out to other lumber companies. Named the "Clyde," this fifteen-ton locomotive was standard gauge with a horizontal boiler and, as with its predecessor, had all eight wheels powered by a chain and sprocket drive.

However, things didn't go well with "Clyde." For one thing the type of steel then available was not of the quality needed to stand the abuse of the drive chains. This discouraging result scrapped plans that Sykes had to begin manufacturing this style of geared locomotive, a patent

for which he had obtained in 1888, the year he moved from Benzinger to Emporium to make his home.

The "Clyde" was rented out and later used by Sykes himself as a switcher at the Keating Summit sawmill in 1899 and at the mill in Danby, Vermont in 1906. The final cut-up didn't come until about 1950 at a siding behind the Conifer, New York sawmill.

Keating Summit Sawmill

As business expanded under capable management, there arose the need for additional expansion capital and a

Keating Summit sawmill with some of the workers' houses nearby.

new corporation. The Emporium Lumber Company was formed in August of 1892 with $30,000 in stock.

The list of officers presented quite an array of Williams and, as it turned out, in-laws. With William L. Sykes as president; William S. Caflisch as general superintendent; William S. Walker of Austin as vice president and eventually sales manager; William T. Turner of Keating Summit as secretary-treasurer; and Evan J. Jones as vice president and general counsel there was formed a dynamic leadership that soon forged ahead of the competitors. Sykes was demonstrating his flair for accumulating needed talent and capital. In time all became related through marriage

except for Turner.

The following year, 1893, a new hardwood sawmill was built at Keating Summit on Portage Creek at the north end of the village and alongside the Pennsylvania Railroad. As with all of the major Sykes' mills, this was a band mill, operating on one side only. William Caflisch was the mill superintendent at Keating Summit, and remained in that capacity after the corporation added additional sawmills.

The Sykes and Caflisch sawmill in Benzinger continued under lease to the Emporium Lumber Company from 1895 to 1897. Available timber became depleted in the area, and the Benzinger mill closed in 1897.

At this point a working alliance was arranged with another larger lumber company that was to reap huge benefits for the Emporium Lumber Company. The Goodyear Lumber Company, then known under the firm name of F. H. and C. W. Goodyear, had been operating large sawmills in Keating Summit and in Austin, and owned large acreages of timberland. But the Goodyears were hemlock manufacturers and not interested in hardwood. Their two mills in Austin were turning out such large volumes that the city became known as "Hemlock City." Along with their expanding lumber manufacturing facilities, the Goodyears had been building an extensive network of logging railroads into the many heavily timbered runs. In 1893, the network was consolidated to form the Buffalo and Susquehanna Railroad.

A working arrangement was established that was ideal for Emporium. The Goodyears would lay the track and remove the hemlock and be followed by Sykes' crew who would log out the remaining hardwood. The Emporium Lumber Company always used their own railroad locomotive and equipment, however.

About once a year, Sykes would call at the Buffalo office

The "Clyde," Sykes' second locomotive at Horton City, Pennsylvania, about 1892. This shop-built engine was also geared by a chain and sprocket drive, but was not very successful.

Emporium's Shay No. 39 on Lyman Run with a Barnhart loader and train of empty log cars. (*Collection of Thomas T. Taber III*)

Typical style of railroad building when logging pikes first reached the Pennsylvania woods. Two parallel lines of squared timbers were laid into notches cut into hefty cross ties and rails spiked on the top of the timbers.

Climax No. 5 with Barnhart loader and short train cleaning up the remnants at a log landing on a typical Pennsylvania "run." (*Collection of Thomas T. Taber III*)

of Frank H. Goodyear to rework the agreement. Before long Goodyear would quickly state that he had the price and that Sykes could arrange all the details. Armed with an agreement to supply his three large mills with a year's supply of forty million board feet, Sykes would then leave and walk diagonally across the street to the Marine Trust and borrow on the strength of the agreement.

There were occasions when similar agreements were worked out, such as the one with the Central Pennsylvania Lumber Company, large hemlock manufacturers.

Railroad Logging in Pennsylvania

Laying a railroad right-of-way up one of the Pennsylvania runs meant a crooked road for there was little choice but to follow the creek bed. This meant there was a rough track not suited to the conventional "rod" locomotive with

its rigid frame. The loggers had the answer, and two common types of geared locomotives, the Shay and the Climax, were put into use by the Pennsylvania loggers to traverse the runs.

The Shay, made by the Lima Locomotive Company in Ohio, never received the popularity in Pennsylvania that it did in the northeast, but was quite effective with its flexible drive shaft along the right side which powered each wheel on that side. The loggers in the Allegheny hills dubbed this practical hard worker a "stemwinder" or "limie." With the smaller Shays, particularly those under

Climax No. 5 in the Hammersley area near Wharton, Pennsylvania. This 50-ton engine was bought new by the Emporium Lumber Company in 1905 and used for forty years before being sold. (*Collection of Thomas T. Taber III*)

Baldwin No. 3, a saddleback locomotive used as a switcher at the Keating Summit mill and later rebuilt into an 0-6-2 and used in New York State on the Grasse River Railroad main line. The young man on the extreme left is Jesse Blesh, later to become the company's master mechanic. (*Collection of Thomas T. Taber III*)

forty tons, the outside line shaft would cause the wheels to climb off the track when under power.

The Climax, on the other hand, was a locally made product, manufactured in Corry, Pennsylvania, and had its greatest popularity in that region. Powered by two cylinders mounted on opposite sides and connected to a central drive shaft, the Climax would hold the track better than the Shay, despite the herky-jerky motion. A Climax would usually out-pull a Shay of equal weight, although the advantage was insignificant with engines over seventy tons.

Emporium showed a preference for the large Shays which overcame the derailment problem with their lower center of gravity, and were much smoother riding than the Climax. During the years of logging the Pennsylvania hills, Emporium's locomotive roster included four Shays and two Climaxes.

These temporary railroads laid up the runs became known as "tram roads" in the lingo of Pennsylvania loggers. Originally built with a base of logs laid down in parallel pairs and joined in fifteen-foot sections, the rails would be spiked lengthwise on top of these logs. As equipment became necessarily a little heavier, ties were used but construction was crude. Most of the major hol-

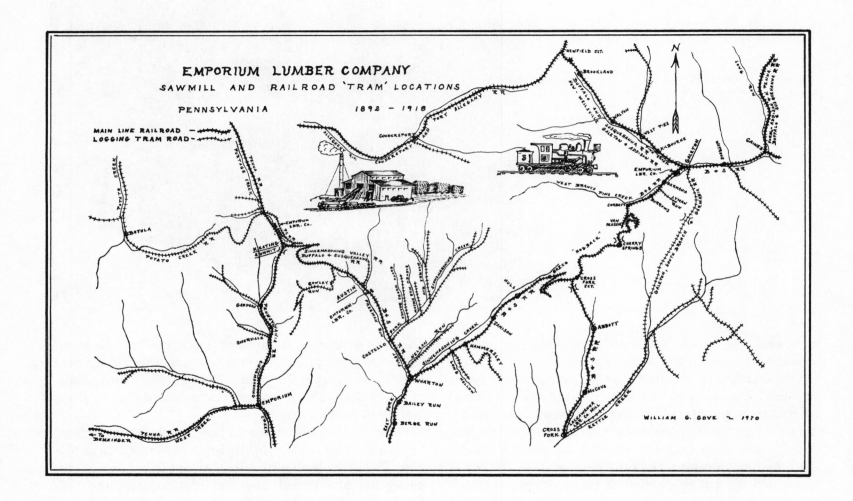

EMPORIUM LUMBER COMPANY
SAWMILL AND RAILROAD 'TRAM' LOCATIONS
PENNSYLVANIA   1892 — 1918

MAIN LINE RAILROAD —
LOGGING TRAM ROAD —

WILLIAM G. GOVE ~ 1970

50

The mill complex at Galeton, Pennsylvania showing sawmill, flooring mill, and wood novelty factory.

lows felt the pounding of steam cylinders.

The normal procedure was to use the geared locomotives on the tram roads, bring the trainload of logs to the siding at the main line, and use a rod locomotive to bring in the train from there to the mill. The term "rod locomotive" refers to the conventional type of steam locomotive with the piston rod powered directly to the drive wheels.

The Emporium Lumber Company brought logs into their new Keating Summit sawmill from quite a wide area, and they employed the many tram roads built and formerly used by the Goodyear Lumber Company. Not many logs actually came from nearby areas. Throughout the twenty years of the operating life of this mill, many logs were brought up from the tram roads off of the B&S

Railroad between Austin and Hull. Log trains rolled out of Sizerville, Cowley Run, and later down the Potato Creek Railroad which the Goodyears built west of Keating Summit in 1907.

Log cars came in from New York over the Pennsylvania Railroad, and in the last years of the Keating Summit operation, logs were transported fifty-five miles over the B&S from the Medix Run area.

The "run in" over the B&S main line was also handled by the Emporium engine, possibly one of the small 0-6-0's or the Baldwin saddle tank that saw frequent service on the Potato Creek Railroad. Clearance would first be obtained by telephone at the tram road junction.

The Keating Summit sawmill had a relatively long and

Baldwin "8," a Forney-type used on the Chicago and South Side elevated railway and exhibited at the 1893 Chicago World's Fair, was used as a "run-in" engine over the B&S Railroad to the Galeton sawmill. (*Collection of Thomas T. Taber III*)

prosperous life, operating two shifts daily and cutting about ten million board feet per year. On May 1, 1901, the mill and five homes burned, taking with it two cars of lumber and damaging a Shay. This was apparently the only Sykes mill ever to burn, and it was soon rebuilt.

Galeton Sawmill

After six prosperous years at Keating Summit, the supply of hardwood timber still seemed endless, and another sawmill came forth. In 1899, a new mill was built in Galeton at the west end of town and on the West Branch of Pine Creek, just west of the B&S Railroad shops. This move was undoubtedly encouraged by Goodyear's purchase of the large Clinton mill in Galeton four years previously.

This also was a single-cut band mill having a cutting capacity of 50,000 board feet per day, and in excess of ten million per year. The saws hummed day and night during the mill's seventeen years.

Hardwood logs for the Emporium mill came in from the tram roads in such nearby locations as Elk Run at Gaines, West Branch, Lyman Run, and Nine Mile Run. One train per day was operated, coming in over the B&S main line.

The train would leave early with twenty to twenty-two cars and start loading by 6 A.M. When loaded it would return home. Loading operations in the narrow runs were greatly simplified when, in about 1894, the Goodyears encouraged development of the Barnhart loader.

The Barnhart, named after the inventor, was a powerful and practical steam loader that found quick acceptance by loggers. It would sit on top of the log cars and pull itself along them on rails built on the cars. After loading a car with five to seven thousand board feet of hardwood, it would secure onto the train with a cable about three cars ahead and then winch itself along with a patented slack pulley. After moving ahead one car, the Barnhart would load the car it had just been sitting on and then continue on, moving back until it reached the end of the train. The Emporium Lumber Company had a number of Barnharts, sometimes as many as four at one time.

It took skill to be an operator, but even then not many could equal Ed Ressler's boast of loading eight hundred logs per day. When he wanted to, Ed could swing the tongs out rapidly and yet lay them gently into the hands of the tong setter. The log would come back in a flurry and set down into place.

The tram roads always produced their share of operating problems due to the rough terrain. Roy Sykes recalled the Shay that broke a coupling up in Lyman Run in 1907. Roy jumped into his favorite Thomas Flyer and took off with two or three lumberjacks in the backseat, headed for Galeton to get a spare part. Before he had gone far he met a team of horses coming up the run, and having no place to pass in the confined area, he steered his hurtling vehicle off into the brush and, after a few jolting jounces, out into the road behind the frightened team. The lumberjacks had a story to tell that night at camp.

Derailments were common but seldom a big problem with a Shay. A "replacer" would be laid in front of the wandering wheel and the Shay would walk gently back onto the rails again.

Apparently all four of the Pennsylvania-operated Shays saw service at the Galeton operation as well as one of the Climaxes. The latter, Climax No. 6, blew up one day when the water supply in the boiler had gotten low and the crew was unaware of the situation because of a closed valve which shut off the level indicator. When they added

The Austin, Pennsylvania sawmill of the Emporium Lumber Company. The main line of the Buffalo & Susquehanna Railroad as it passed the millpond and yard. (*Collection of Thomas T. Taber III*)

a fresh supply of cold water to the overheated boiler, they had trouble. One crewman by the name of Hazelton was killed.

One of these Shays, No. 10 (later No. 40), was the best and largest of the many Shays eventually to be numbered among Sykes' possessions. This was a 92-ton, three-truck Shay originally built in 1902 and purchased by Emporium in 1910 from the Lackawanna Lumber Company of Cross Fork, Pennsylvania. Future years of expansion by the Sykes' hardwood domain were to see much in the way of rugged service from this workhorse.

Included among the "run-in" engines for main line service at Galeton was a Baldwin 0-4-4-T Forney that formerly had seen service on an elevated railroad and was believed to have been exhibited at the 1893 Chicago Worlds' Fair. Emporium maintained their railroad repair shops at Galeton, probably not coincidentally, as the big B&S Railroad shops were nearby.

For many years the Goodyear Lumber Company had been operating two large hemlock mills in Austin to handle their large timber cut in the area, sawing six days a week around the clock. South of these mills, three-quarters of a mile down Freeman Run from the center of Austin, was located the band mill of A. G. Lyman, who, it is rumored, did not want to handle the large hardwood volume the Goodyears had to offer. At any rate, the Emporium Lumber Company bought the mill in 1901, along with another in Portageville, New York, which was not being operated at the time.

Logs came from the runs northeast of Wharton, in the region where many trainloads had been coming out for some time to the Keating Summit mill. A tram was built into the Hammersley area out of Jamison and access was gained to many small hollows and runs. The No. 5 Climax

worked the Hammersley area and was kept at the engine-house in Jamison. The run-in engine from Jamison to Austin was No. 41 Baldwin, a fantail Consolidated 2-8-0.

During their twenty-five years of railroad logging, Sykes and crew owned and operated fourteen locomotives. A brief rundown showed four Shays, two Climaxes, and six rod locomotives, as well as their two homemade locomotives. Toward the end of the Pennsylvania operations, Emporium did have to construct several miles of its own track.

With the addition of the Austin sawmill there were three single band mills, and the company's letterhead could proudly boast a "combined annual capacity of 40,000,000 board feet of band-sawed hardwood." Throughout this prosperous period, the main office remained at Keating Summit, home of general superintendent William Caflisch. Corporation officers didn't change.

The cutting practices in those days were severe, and the hills were thoroughly denuded as both softwood and hardwood were removed. With such rapid consumption and utilization there naturally had to be an end to timber resources; before many years it became evident.

The Hammersley cut, which began about 1905, was the last big cut undertaken jointly by Goodyear and Emporium, and seeing the handwriting on the wall, Sykes was looking elsewhere. The Allegheny hills were now only brown with slash and Emporium needed hills alive with green gold.

Their hungry eyes looked northeastward toward up-state New York and Vermont. Some of the corporation's officers and their relatives had been up in the Adirondacks on deer hunting excursions and reports came back of a veritable paradise of untouched hardwoods. It wasn't long before the Sykes' fortune and initiative were soon at work in this direction.

As the timber gradually played out in Pennsylvania, activities slowed down, although not all at once. The Keating Summit mill closed down in 1913 after twenty-years of operation and the Austin mill closed the same year after twelve years under the ownership of the Emporium Lumber Company.

It wasn't until after the far-flung Sykes' domain had begun to operate elsewhere that the Galeton mill closed in 1916, climaxing seventeen years of operating day and night. The mill sat idle for many years after that and was eventually occupied by the Patterson Lumber Company.

After two disastrous fires in 1960 and 1969 they operated a completely new hardwood sawmill on the same site for many years.

Now, with Galeton closed, all that was left in Pennsylvania for this hardwood king of olden days was about 30,000 acres of denuded land which remained in company ownership. All concerned had taken families, relatives, friends, and memories, and departed for the Adirondack region of New York. This hopefully would be the big move that would keep the Sykes' hardwood domain alive. This would possibly lead to even greater heights for the hardwood king.

A small saddletank handles the train on a landing at the base of a log slide.

3

The Emporium Forestry Company

by William Gove

New York and Danby, Vermont

At about the same time that land purchases began in New York, a large amount of acreage became available in the lower portion of the Green Mountains of Vermont. In 1906, a tract of upward of 35,000 acres, plus a sawmill, was purchased by Sykes for about $500,000. The sawmill location was near the village of Danby.

This bargain was picked up from the estate of Silas O. Griffith of Danby, a well-known Vermont lumberman. Griffith has gone into the annals of history as a real character and a shrewd businessman who made his fortune on charcoal and lumber manufacture.

He had built this sawmill at the southern end of Mt. Tabor township near the winding Otter Creek. Connection to the outside commercial world was by means of a branch spur from the Rutland Railroad, then the Bennington and Rutland. Built after Griffith had ceased operating his renowned "old job" mill complex on Big Branch Brook, this mill became known to local residents as the "south end."

Sykes kept the sawmill operating for ten years, man-aged by Nelson C. Nichols. It was not a large mill, especially by the standards of that era. The sawmill had a circular headsaw and a No. 2 Lane forty-foot carriage capable of cutting ten to twelve thousand board feet per day of both spruce and hardwood. A lath machine, a bolter saw, and four lathes for turning chair legs made up the remaining machinery.

William Sykes was a railroad logger, so a pike was constructed to service the "south end" mill. The three-mile standard gauge line was built in a northerly direction along the westerly base of the steep Green Mountain range, but actually provided access to only a small percentage of the acreage they had acquired. A double switchback was employed to overcome a steep grade about half way out.

Only one locomotive was used, the homemade geared engine named "Clyde." The Sykes also had four or five log cars, but used only two at a time because of the steep grades.

The local folks called it the UH&DS—"Uphill and Damn Steep"—and it must have been a risky operation

The locomotive "Clyde" No. 2, at the mill log dump, Danby, Vermont sawmill, 1907.

The Danby, Vermont sawmill. Most of the crew brought their children out for this 1907 photo.

with only hand brakes on the log cars. The only known accident occurred when a crooked and partly-peeled birch log slipped out of the wrapper chain on the car and came forward into the locomotive cab, stripping off a few pipes but, fortunately, no heads.

This sawmill, never a big part of the Sykes' empire, was closed down in 1916 after ten years of operation. Much of the timber was never cut. About 1918, Martin Brown, of the Parker Young Company, tried to purchase the valuable tract for a reported one million dollars, knowing that the New England Power Company would soon be buying up the Deerfield River watershed. Sykes turned down the offer because he was skeptical of Parker Young bonds which were to cover a large portion of the price. Most of the land is now part of the Green Mountain National Forest.

In 1905, the Emporium Lumber Company began large land purchases in the Adirondacks, purchases that would continue for the next thirty-eight years and amass, at its peak ownership, in excess of 125,000 acres of prime hardwood timber.

The first New York purchase was one of 18,000 acres in the township of Clare in 1905. This was on the northern edge of the Adirondacks and appears to have been compatible with the company's original intention to build a sawmill at Canton, New York. From there the logs would be hauled by a logging railroad in a westerly direction to junction with the New York Central Railroad, and thus routed to Canton.

William L. Sykes was a good organizer, and it was soon evident in his surveillance that Canton was not the place for the sawmill. Land purchases would become easier to the east, and the obvious area for a mill location would be in the upper watershed of the Grasse River. He continued to purchase land in that area.

Conifer, New York

Land purchases in the Adirondacks, begun in 1905, continued for another five years, and then definite preparations were made to construct a new village and sawmill facility. At a point on Dead Creek, a tributary of the Raquette River and about ten miles west of Tupper Lake, near Piercefield, Sykes and his group built the village of Conifer. Their Pennsylvania fortunes were gradually to shift to this area.

The Conifer site was purchased from the small firm of George A. McCoy & Son in 1910. McCoy had erected a few log buildings and was in the process of putting up a circular sawmill, in preparation of logging a nearby 35,000-acre tract for International Paper Company. Sykes sent in a crew which set up camp in the small cluster of log buildings and soon went to work erecting a sawmill that was worthy of the company's reputation. A contractor by the name of A. S. Heltman was brought in to build many of the residences which were to make up the village surrounding the sawmill.

The mill began operation in October 1911. For thirty-seven and one-half years it operated steadily under Emporium ownership at a production rate of eight to ten million board feet per year. In all, a total of close to 350 million.

To handle the New York operations, William Sykes and associates formed a new corporation in 1912, the Emporium Forestry Company. Control was still primarily in the same hands, but now W. L. Sykes' three sons had progressed to the point of assuming leadership. The slate of officers of the new corporation read as follows: George W. Sykes, president and general superintendent; E. J. Jones, vice president and general counsel; Roy O. Sykes, vice president and sales manager; W. Clyde Sykes, treasurer;

The original log structures at Conifer when William L. Sykes purchased the site in 1910. The buildings behind the Emporium crew are, from left to right: the barn, bunkhouse, lounge and dining room, and cook shack. Orrin Prince, scaler, is in the left foreground.

The Conifer sawmill when first constructed in 1911.

and Arthur L. Owen, secretary.

William L. Sykes and William S. Caflisch, the company patriarchs, were still on the scene, however, guiding and directing their new venture. Caflisch was a gruff individual who was all business and often bickered with Sykes. He was a popular man, though, and would jump right in and work with the men, but is reputed to have used a little physical force on occasions when a man was seen slacking off.

The occasion is recalled when Caflisch was working with a crew shoveling gravel along the shoulder of the railroad bed. The locomotive of the work train was standing idle, and noticing the fireman with nothing to do,

Caflisch called up, "Pardner, (he called everyone Pardner) there's an extra shovel down here." The fireman's reply that he wasn't hired to do that kind of work did not set well with Caflisch, and when the man returned to the office that night he found himself temporarily without a job. Only considerable pleading got him his job back. He later became an engineer.

W. L. Sykes, in contrast, was one who would take moments off from work and talk at length with an employee if the latter showed an interest in the company's activities and in advancing. At times Sykes could be quite long-winded, he loved to talk about trees and forestry.

The first logging for the new mill was done just east of

The original log structures at Conifer, which William L. Sykes purchased in 1910, were used to house the Emporium crew until the village was built.

Conifer, and for the first few years, until about 1920, lumbering was concentrated in that region. In 1913, two years after the sawmill opened, construction began on a railroad which would eventually reach out to the extensive timberland ownerships. The Emporium Lumber Company had accumulated an imposing roster of railroad equipment while logging the countless "runs" that they had denuded in Pennsylvania. It was only to be expected that a first-rate railroad would be part of their plans in New York from the very beginning.

The first rails were laid up Dead Creek, south of Conifer, followed by a line that extended westward over to the Silver Brook area. This was in the same year that the Penn-sylvania sawmills in Keating Summit and Austin shut down, and rolling stock began to arrive at Conifer. The link with the outside world was forged at a point just over a mile east of Conifer where the company railroad junctioned with the Adirondack Division of the New York Central (the former Mohawk and Malone). This junction became known as Childwold. Emporium's railroad was standard gauge, as it had been in Pennsylvania.

In that same year the railroad was extended the sixteen miles to Cranberry Lake, a beautiful and, until then, inaccessible Adirondack lake which afforded a summer resort for the few fortunate ones. Emporium had previously purchased an inn at the village on the north end of the lake.

An early view of the Conifer, New York saw-mill, with railroad log dump in the foreground.

The principal men of the Emporium Lumber Company posed in front of the Conifer sawmill. From left to right: Arthur L. Owen, J. C. Schumberger, Joshua Sykes (father of W. L.), William L. Sykes, William C. Caflisch, Evan J. Jones, Frank P. Sykes, William S. Walker, William T. Turner (front), 1906.

64

Italian laborers constructing the Grasse River Railroad along the north shore of Silver Lake in 1913.

Track-laying crew on the "north tram." Note the slab wood used for fill and the practice of shimming the crude ties with wood blocks.

This portion of the railroad was to become a main line and was sturdily built, a care not extended to many of the logging branches or trams.

Using work crews made up of Italian immigrants, the temporary lines were often made by laying ties and rails right on the ground, dumping fill on top, then tamping down the gravel, and jacking up the track where necessary. Often the roadbed was built on whole logs or trees, using species of little value such as hemlock. Ties would be hewn in the woods and thrown into place, with a wooden block used to patch up where the rail wouldn't seat properly. A cold-dip creosote treatment was applied in the case of ties from which longer use was expected. The main lines, Childwold to Cranberry Lake and the

north tram which extended over thirty miles north from the Dodge Brook "Y" at Cranberry, were to give almost thirty years of hard service.

The Conifer mill was now in full swing, keeping about seventy-five employees busy under the direction of mill superintendent, Clinton Fuller. Included among the duties of yard superintendent, Paul Thomas, was running the expanding dry kiln facilities which were so necessary even then in the trade. George Sykes designed the first Conifer kiln, a railroad kiln that held six cars with a total capacity of 90,000 board feet.

Timberland purchases were continuing in the area around Cranberry Lake and in the vast region to the north. Although buying continued until 1943, the primary land

Alco-Schenectady No. 2, a Mogul, was the last locomotive to be purchased by Emporium.

Number 68, a Schenectady purchased in 1923 and an ex-New York Central, saw many years of use on the Grasse River line.

purchases were made by the year 1920. Large tracts surrounding Cranberry Lake were purchased from International Paper Company after they had logged them, in some cases twice, for the softwood pulpwood. In time the ownership was to total 125,000 acres or about 190 to 195 square miles.

The Grasse River Railroad

After the railroad had been completed to Cranberry Lake village, an opportunity became apparent—a source of additional revenues by means of passenger and mail service. Thus, the Grasse River Railroad was born in 1915, and incorporated as a common carrier to traverse the sixteen mile course from Childwold to Cranberry Lake that had originally been built for hauling logs. With the advent of this development, the records of the locomotives and operating costs on the logging branches were kept separate from those of the Grasse River Railroad.

As in Pennsylvania, the geared locomotives, the Shays and the Climaxes, were used on the logging train roads and rod locomotives employed on the main line to run the train of log cars into the sawmill and perform switching duties. Of the fourteen locomotives owned in Pennsylvania, nine were brought up to the Adirondacks and, with the later addition of twelve more locomotives purchased while in New York, it meant a roster of twenty-one locomotives during the many years at Conifer. The total roster for both states numbered twenty-six. Only two were ever bought new, both Climaxes.

There were eleven "rod engines" of three different makes—Schenectady, Brooks, and Baldwin. There were eight of the favored Shays, although three were never used, and two Climax engines. The normal procedure was to keep about three rod locomotives in operating condi-

Building of the Grasse River Railroad, an elevated section being set on pilings. (*Collection of Pat McKenney*)

tion to service the Grasse River line.

As recalled by Pat McKenney, who worked on the railroad, Shay No. 40 was not only the largest locomotive they ever had, but also the best. It was a powerful brute of ninety-two tons that was built in 1902 and scrapped in 1962 after being used on the Elk River Coal and Lumber Company line in West Virginia.

The Grasse River line had a single combination passenger and baggage coach for passenger service, and for the first few years revenues exceeded expenses. For about ten years prior to the inception of the Grasse River Railroad, summer residents had been able to arrive at Cranberry

Number 2, with a couple of boxcars, en route from Conifer to the junction at Childwold, is viewed crossing Pleasant Lake Stream.

Lake via the New York Central to Benson Mines, and then the Rich brothers' railroad into Wanakena at the lower end of the lake. However, this service ceased in 1914 after the Rich brothers shut down the Wanakena sawmill.

Now it became convenient, as the summer season arrived, for the affluent to arrive at Childwold on the New York Central-Montreal Express and make connections for Cranberry Lake. Arriving at the early hour of 5:30 A.M., the departing passengers would rub their sleepy eyes and search for that little Grasse River locomotive and her single coach. But her frequent late arrivals would make it an eager wait for these folks not accustomed to such early awakenings. Anticipation for the coming season at the lake would soon turn impatience into the joyful realization that they were about to have that unique ride on the Grasse River, a joy they had often thought about at their winter homes in the city.

After departing the station at Childwold, the Grasse River train would usually stop at Conifer for about an hour, and the passengers were given an opportunity to enjoy a breakfast at the Conifer Inn next to the depot. A sumptuous serving of cereal, bacon, eggs, and thick pancakes was provided to local workers for fifty cents, but of course, to traveling folks the price was one dollar. Many suspected a holdup game, but after all, this was part of the summer experience to dream about next winter.

The early morning jaunt from Conifer on to Cranberry Lake was truly an adventure to delight any youngster who had spent the winter in an urban environment. Squeals of excitement filled the little coach as deer or heron were spotted in the marshes along the Grasse River Flow, or whenever the engineer had to whistle a deer off the track. On arrival at the long-awaited destination, the coach would be left at the edge of the lake while the

Shay No. 40, a 92-ton locomotive, was proclaimed to be the largest and best engine Emporium owned among its roster of twenty-six locomotives. The company used it for forty years. (*Collection of Pat McKenney*)

A New York Central passenger train pauses at the depot at Childwold, the point where the Grasse River Railroad began its sixteen-mile length westward to Cranberry Lake.

The Grasse River Railroad arrived daily at Cranberry Lake village with a complement of one coach and a few empty log cars.

The Grasse River Railroad's No. 2 passing the depot and store in Conifer en route to Childwold in 1949. (*Photo by Philip Hastings*)

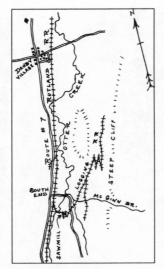

Danby, Vermont sawmill and
railroad, 1908-1916.

The Emporium Forestry Company and the
Grasse River Railroad. (*Maps by William Gove*)

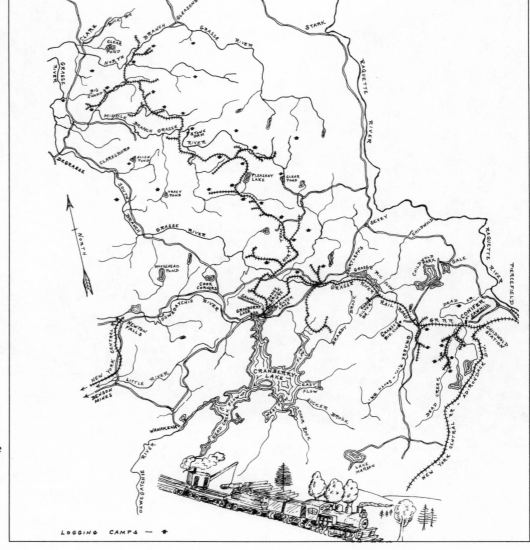

engine went off to perform a few switching duties.

In 1922, two trains a day were being run in each direction, except on Sunday, with a traveling time of a little over an hour from Childwold to Cranberry Lake. That is an hour when one of the convenient meal stops wasn't made at the Conifer Inn. Roy O. Sykes, William Sykes' youngest, was the superintendent of the railroad.

One of the Shay geared locomotives could be found operating on the network of logging lines north of Cranberry Lake and would bring down twelve to twenty-two loaded log cars and leave them on a siding near the Dodge Brook "Y," a half-mile east of the Cranberry Lake terminal. This "north tram" extended for thirty miles up to the north end of Clare township and was a long, six-hour trip for a Shay to return with a trainload from the far end.

From the Cranberry Lake siding the log train would be taken into the Conifer sawmill by the Grasse River Railroad locomotive. The usual makeup was to push the log cars ahead and to pull behind the coach and whatever boxcars of lumber there were from the Cranberry Lake sawmill. The trip into Conifer took another hour.

The one hundred fifty or more log cars were made by the company in their own shop and featured a trip chain device that was patented by Caflisch. Loading was done with the Barnhart loaders, traveling on top of the cars as they loaded the car from behind. Ed Ressler and Archie Pollard are remembered as expert operators who could place the tongs carefully where needed and yet with unmatched speed. Most trainloads were made up of twenty-two cars, each with 5,000 to 7,000 feet of logs. Couplers were link and pin and the brakes were hand set, using a bar called a "Jim Crow."

Climax No. 44 on the "north tram."

Maple and birch logs awaiting the loader along the "north tram." (*Photo by William L. Distin*)

Moving the train into position for loading is locomotive No. 43, a small Brooks that the company owned for seven years before selling in 1918.

The Barnhart loader busy loading a string of empties behind Shay No. 51.

Cranberry Lake Sawmill

Lumber markets were good during World War I, and the Emporium Forestry Company deemed it advisable to build a second Adirondack sawmill. In 1917, a large, double band mill was built on the northwest shore of Silver Lake, on the edge of Cranberry Lake village, and operations were begun in September of that year. The intention was to saw a considerable amount of softwood on one side using two band headsaws.

This mill was said to be the best that Sykes ever built, but as it turned out, it also proved to be the most expensive to operate. Arthur Owen, superintendent, ran this facility with the latest in machinery such as a twin band re-saw and a jumpsaw trimmer. Production was almost double that of Conifer, and during its ten years of operation it turned out at least two hundred million board feet of lumber. At times there would be twelve million board

feet on sticks in the yard.

Although the mill did saw some spruce, pine, and hemlock, hardwood predominated. Many spruce logs were shipped out as "fiddlebutts" (high quality logs used in the making of sounding boards for musical instruments); a great deal of the softwood was put into pulpwood. In contrast to Conifer, Cranberry Lake had no dry kiln or flooring mill.

The following year, 1918, their last Pennsylvania mill at Galeton closed its doors, and the company's manufacturing efforts were now solely within the Adirondacks, the Danby, Vermont mill having been shut down in 1916. At the close of the Keating Summit mill, the general office had been moved to Utica, New York, and then, in 1926, to Conifer where it remained. The Woods Department headquarters was located at Cranberry Lake. Loren Silliman spent many years at Emporium as an office manager of outstanding loyalty.

A large yellow birch log is swung into place in front of Shay No. 39 as W. L. Sykes proudly points out its virtues to his visitors.

75

Logging Activities

Almost all of the logs sawn by the Emporium Forestry Company came from their own timberlands. Frank Sykes, a cousin of William Sykes, was the first woods superintendent in New York, later followed by his son, Chester W. Sykes.

One of the more interesting inventions developed by Frank Sykes was a portable log slide which he patented. Remembering the old days in Pennsylvania when horses pulled trains of logs along a slide built of logs, Frank built a slide that could be transported and assembled in eight-foot sections. Each section had three pieces to form a trough, with the sides tapered and with slots on the end to piece the sections together. A train of logs would be pulled long distances along the slide by a team of horses, one on each side of the slide. A Cletrac tractor was later

The Cranberry Lake sawmill, the finest ever built by Sykes and company.

used on the slide instead of horses. The uphill and level portions were greased often, the company buying slide oil by the barrel.

When the areas purchased from the International Paper Company east and south of Cranberry Lake were logged off in the 1920s, the logs were brought up the lake in rafts and loaded on log cars on the Grasse River Railroad at the head of the lake. Rafts were made by laying four or five fifty-foot spruce logs parallel in the water, and fastening the front ends, at intervals, along a sixteen-foot log. The hardwood logs were then placed crossways on the raft by a Barnhart loader which was placed on a float where it could reach the logs piled on the shore. The tugboat, *Wallace*, would be seen pulling about ten of these rafts up the lake from the Sucker Brook area, Chair Rock Flow, or possibly West Flow. One trip would be enough to fill a trainload. They would load the cars on a trestle built out into the lake, using another Barnhart. This operation was

A horse-drawn railroad used at Wheeler Mountain by Emporium during early logging days. Crew poses at the landing just above the second camp. Note the wide-flanged wheels which ran on log rails. (*Collection of Paul Thomas*)

76

The log slide, patented by Frank Sykes, in use in the Dead Creek area. The hardwood logs were attached end to end with grapples, and pulled along the oiled slide trough by a team of horses.

Loading rafts with hardwood logs on Cranberry Lake. The Barnhart loader is setting on a float and the raft, made of long softwood logs, can be seen in the foreground. (*Collection of Pat McKenney*)

A Linn tractor with a train of eight sleds of hardwood logs. (*Collection of Pat McKenney*)

77

one of the many jobs ably supervised by Henry Cope, an excellent woodsman, who drove logs on the Connecticut River and on Pennsylvania's Susquehanna River before coming to the Adirondacks for Sykes.

It might be pointed out that Emporium was not the first to raft logs down Cranberry Lake. International Paper Company jobbers had built log slides on Indian Mountain years before, and sent logs speeding down the hill into South Flow and Chair Rock Flow. From there huge booms of softwood sawlogs and pulpwood were towed up the lake by *Old Ironclad* and sent on down the Oswegatchie River. It took two days to haul the half-acre of logs in the boom six miles down the lake.

As Emporium was logging their hardwood, softwood pulpwood was also being cut. During the 1920s pulpwood was hauled down to Cranberry Lake on the railroad and dumped into the lake, then driven down the Oswegatchie River to the Newton Falls paper mill. A few years later the four-foot wood was being railroaded in the other direction. Stacked in open-topped rack cars, it was hauled east to the International Paper Company's pulp mill in Piercefield, traversing the last two miles over the New York Central from Childwold. In 1930-31, the legendary John E. Johnston rafted long pulpwood up Cranberry Lake to a jackworks and conveyor where it was loaded onto the Grasse River Railroad, destined for Piercefield.

In some of the areas not accessible from a railroad branch the company used Linn tractors, of which they had four. The large expanse east of Cranberry Lake was logged with the Linns, each hauling six or seven large sleds and making the run either to the Grasse River Club Station on the railroad or all the way into the Cranberry Lake sawmill. The Linn was one of the earliest types of woods tractor, somewhat like a gasoline-powered Lombard with crawler tracks in the rear and a set of runners in the front for steering. The results were excellent in deep snow.

The nature of the logging activities changed in the 1930s as a swing-over was made from company crews to contract logging for the most part. The woods superintendent at this time was Harry Van Horn, remembered for the sad misfortune he had in 1934 when he threw down some dynamite caps and was killed. Another to be remembered for his supervision of the high production woodland operations is Victor Noelk, one of the many who came up during the move from Pennsylvania.

Railroad Shop

At Conifer, the Emporium Forestry Company had an outstanding railroad shop that could rebuild a locomotive completely. Jesse Blesh, a Pennsylvanian, served in the shop as master mechanic for many years, a position later held by Ray Zenger who resided in Conifer at the time.

Repair work was, of course, in constant demand. Log cars had to be continually repaired or new ones built. The shop crew built their own wood frame railroad "trucks." It's to the credit of both the shop crew and operating crews that neither the Grasse River Railroad nor the logging railroad ever had a major accident, which was quite unusual.

The shop crew, as well as the operating crew, preferred the Shay geared locomotive to its counterpart, the Climax. The working parts and gears were all accessible along the right side of the engine and maintenance was easy. The biggest complaint was that snow would pack into the exposed bevel gears on the face of the wheel, soak up the grease, and cause the gears to clatter loudly.

W. L. Sykes was a man who loved railroad machinery

The Conifer enginehouse with Shay No. 51 in for repairs. Master mechanic Ray Zenger is in the center. (*Photo by Philip Hastings*)

The remains of the enginehouse fire at Conifer in the early 1920s.

and felt an overpowering need to collect and save spare parts. As one might suspect, this created quite a junk pile near the railroad shop. Once when Sykes was on a trip to Utica, his sons took the opportunity to clean house a little and sold a considerable amount to a junk dealer. Quickly loading it on flatcars, they had it on the way south before their father returned. But father, returning home on the New York Central, spotted the good-looking collection of spare parts loaded on flatcars, sitting on a siding, and im-

mediately wired the junkman that he would purchase the parts, possibly unaware they were originally his.

Among the devices to be credited to the originality of William Sykes and his crew was a patented flexible stay bolt to go between the sheets in the firebox of the boiler.

The ingenuity of William Sykes was apparently inherited by his youngest son, Roy, who spent many hours in the shop, along with the mechanics, building various types of motor cars for service on the Grasse River Rail-

80

Motor car No. 11 with Rob Mills at the controls, the converted White bus used to carry passengers and mail from the station at Childwold to Cranberry Lake.

road. It was costly to run steam on the sixteen-mile run, with at times hardly more than a couple of bags of mail, so cheaper operating rolling stock was always being experimented with.

One experiment was Roy's 1905 "Thomas Flyer" automobile. It was rebuilt, in 1916, with railroad wheels and a chain drive, and called the No. 2 "Rolliam." About the same time there was No. 1, the "Will Roll Some," an old Pullman car powered with a 100-horsepower Sterling engine that was mounted on posts resting on truck pedestals. Roy spoke proudly of this innovation which cut down on the car vibration. She carried both passengers and mail.

Number 4 motor car came forth when one of the small

Baldwin locomotives had her boiler removed and a Sterling gasoline engine installed. Many still remember No. 11, an old White bus that was rebuilt with double trucks and chain drive on the rear truck. Some called her the "Jumping Goose." Number 12 was an old rail interurban car that had at least two different engines installed. It was large but economical and carried freight and passengers for ten years.

The shop was equipped to convert the locomotives to burn either coal or oil. Because of the serious 1908 fires in the Adirondacks, many started by the railroads, the state adopted regulations, in 1916, empowering the Conservation Commission to prevent coal-burning locomotives from operating during the fire season. Each spring the

Motor car No. 11 patiently waits in a snowstorm at the junction at Childwold for the southbound New York Central mail train. (*Photo by Philip Hastings*)

company would receive official notice that coal-burners were to cease operating until further notification. The Shays were all coal-burners, exclusively, so were hampered at times. Fuel for motive power on the Grasse River Railroad was switched over to oil.

On occasion, the coal-burners were allowed to run if an inspector were to follow fifteen minutes behind on a speeder and look for fires. Ray Zenger fondly remembers this chore because he took along his fishing pole and made short stops at a few good holes along the way, including an occasional private fishing ground such as the Grasse River Club.

Emporium had only one serious forest fire in New York, quite a contrast to the constant forest fires they experienced in Pennsylvania. In 1941, the Grasse River Flow and Club were swept by fire which put quite a scare into the inhabitants of Conifer as they could view the flames down the right-of-way.

In 1926, the Emporium Forestry Company revealed plans to extend the Grasse River Railroad further west. Intentions were to build westerly from the north side of Silver Pond and along the north bank of the Oswegatchie River, crossing the river one mile south of Cook's Corners and continuing westerly either to Benson Mines or Newton Falls. This would, of course, provide a through rail connection in the northwestern Adirondacks, tapping the same junction once used by the Rich Lumber Company's Cranberry Lake Railroad.

In November of that year, the Emporium Forestry Company placed $900,000 of bonds up for sale to finance construction of the addition. The company placed 86,000 acres of timberland as mortgage security, and W. L. Sykes signed the bonds at the Northern New York Trust Company office. Either the money was not raised, or the

Rob Mills picks up the mail at Childwold in preparation for his return to Conifer in the speeder, motor car No. 11.

Motor car No. 12, a converted rail interurban car, was used for about ten years.

depression discouraged further activity as none of this construction ever began.

The New York operations were never as profitable for Sykes and associates as had been the three large Pennsylvania sawmills. Railroad operations were more expensive in the Adirondacks, as there was no track built in advance.

The Grasse River Railroad never proved to be a big moneymaker. Lumber manufacturing costs were great, and the cost of maintaining a village the size of Conifer was stupendous, justified only by the fact that in no other way could one hundred employees readily be available. The Emporium Forestry Company owned all of the homes and other buildings except the school building. Church was kept in the school basement.

George Sykes, oldest son of W. L., acted as general manager of the Emporium Forestry Company and proved to

be quite capable, admitted to even by those who disliked him. He was outspoken, but his word was good. William Caflisch was general manager in Pennsylvania and also at the time of the move to New York. However, Caflisch died in April of 1917, a death surrounded by tragic circumstances because most of his immediate family were killed in a railroad accident en route to his funeral. George Sykes stepped into his shoes.

As the depression years came on, the lumber markets subsided, but the company stayed. Decreasing sales meant less production, however, and the costly operating sawmill at Cranberry Lake had to go. On April 1, 1927, this latest in northeastern sawmills produced its last board. Some of the machinery was later moved to Conifer.

In time George Sykes found that it was not as easy to borrow operating capital on the strength of land ownership as it had been at the height of his father's career. The company had its "ups and downs" financially and was "land poor" at times. In 1930, Emporium began to sell off some of the cutover timberland holdings with large land sales to the Tri-River Power Corporation and the State of New York. Almost half of the land was sold during the depression years.

Much of the accessible timber had been picked over when, in 1941, death overtook the hardwood king, William L. Sykes. Railroad logging up on the "north tram" ceased about this time and some of the rail began to be lifted. Railroad construction had continued until about 1937, with just under one hundred miles of track laid.

After years of hard use the rails had worn considerably and, in many places, had spread beyond standard gauge width. This usually didn't present a problem for the wide "tires" or drive wheels of the Shay geared locomotives, but when Shay No. 40 was sold to a logging line in West Virginia in 1950, it had to be delivered on a flatcar. The wheels were too wide to go through the track frogs on the main line. This track condition once prompted George Sykes to remark to the president of the New York Central Railroad, a personal friend, that Emporuim's sixteen-mile Grasse River Railroad may not be as long as the New York Central's eleven thousand-mile system, but it was definitely wider.

Thirty years of railroad logging now came to an end on Sykes' Adirondack properties. No longer was the roar of steam to be heard across the tamarack swamps or over the knolls of birch and maple. No longer were the Emporium Forestry Company woods camps to vibrate with activity during the winter months. No longer did the loggers come up Cranberry Lake in a motorboat from camps on the Edger Tract, eager for a Saturday night at the Columbian Inn where they could carouse all night and then sleep it

Grasse River Railroad dispatcher issues an order for locomotive No. 2 to "run extra" from Conifer to Childwold, December, 1949. (*Photo by Philip Hastings*)

off out in the grass.

The third and last major land sale was to the Draper Corporation in 1945. This was a neat package of almost 72,000 acres which included some areas still not cut over

85

Rail bus No. 11 has met New York Central train No. 2 at Childwold on a snowy December 23, 1949. (*Photo by Philip Hastings*)

for hardwood. It's not hard to understand why Draper felt this to be an opportunity. But now, despite the objections of some corporation members, Emporium had split its assets of the manufacturing facilities with its source of raw material. Ever since the wheels had begun to turn, in 1911, at the Conifer mill, the company had supplied almost all of the logs from its own lands. Now logs had to be procured outside for delivery by trucks or via the New York Central Railroad from more distant points.

Costs were rising, and the Sykes were losing their enthusiasm to continue. After two full generations in the hardwood dynasty, there was no one in the third generation with a desire to keep alive the Emporium name. Internal disagreements clouded future direction.

The Grasse River Railroad, for many years now a drain on corporate profits, had to go next, and the Adirondacks lost a source of many fond memories. The rail on the remainder of the "north tram" road was taken up soon after Draper Corporation bought the property in 1945, and, in 1948, the rail on the Grasse River line was taken up from Cranberry Lake village east to a point about one mile west of Conifer village. This left an imposing roadbed of precisely two miles for the Grasse River from Conifer to Childwold, plus sidings.

There were still about eight locomotives sitting around, mostly unused, but even those in operating condition didn't run steam much longer under Emporium ownership. During World War II, the Conifer mill had been sawing lumber under a manufacturing agreement with the Heywood-Wakefield Company, and in 1949, when this large furniture manufacturer from Gardner, Massachusetts offered to buy the mill, the Sykes were unanimous in the desire to "get out of it."

In April of that year the deeds were signed, conveying

The switch still isn't set for No. 68 in the Conifer yard. (*Photo by Philip Hastings*)

Cleaning the switch points at Conifer during a storm, No. 2 and Shay No. 40 in the background, 1949. (*Photo by Philip Hastings*)

all of Conifer village, including the sawmill and the re-maining two-mile vestige of the railroad, but only about seventy acres of land in the vicinity of the village. After sixty-seven years of continual operation and seven different sawmill locations, the dynasty built by the hardwood king, William L. Sykes, had splintered and passed into new hands.

In September of 1950, soon after the sale to Heywood-Wakefield, the corporation of Emporium Forestry Company was dissolved, and the remainder of the property was turned over to the original corporation, the Emporium Lumber Company. A small office was still maintained, until 1971 at Cranberry Lake, in the only building left remaining at the sawmill location. Loren Silliman kept the fires burning and tended to whatever business might transpire regarding a few land holdings still held in Pennsylvania, Vermont, and New York.

Heywood-Wakefield Ownership

Heywood-Wakefield rebuilt the sawmill into a unit much more efficient than the former mill, and capable of sawing twelve million board feet per year. New equipment was installed such as an eight-foot band mill, Prescott carriage, Prescott band re-saw, and a jumpsaw trimmer built by Paul Thomas. The outmoded overhead lumber docks were removed and a new sorting system built.

The future had a rosy glow for the inhabitants of Conifer, with mill employment now up to one hundred fifty. Many of the old Emporium supervisory personnel were kept on, including Loren Silliman as superintendent and Victor Noelk in charge of log procurement. Roy Sykes came with them to handle lumber sales. But log costs had now risen excessively, and it wasn't "like it was" during Emporium's days.

Grasse River No. 68 at Childwold, September 1949. (*Photo by Philip Hastings*)

The Grasse River Railroad (what was left of it) had a facelift also. The remaining steam locomotives were either sold or scrapped and, in 1950, a new forty-five ton General Electric diesel locomotive was purchased. This little engine performed admirably for the next few years as carloads of lumber were taken down to the junction at the station at Childwold and flatcars loaded with logs

The storm has cleared and No. 2 prepares to take on water at Conifer, 1949. (*Photo by Philip Hastings*)

The Conifer sawmill about 1955, after being rebuilt by the Heywood-Wakefield Company. (*Photo by Paul S. Davis*)

brought back to Conifer when the New York Central delivered them at the siding. The year 1953 saw fifty million board feet of logs and lumber moved in and out of the operating area with the aid of their rail-mounted diesel cranes. Included here were 725 outbound cars of lumber. (This diesel locomotive could still be seen operating in the Franconia Manufacturing Company's yard in Lincoln, New Hampshire until 1972.)

The Heywood-Wakefield Company probably enjoyed the ownership of their little railroad more than any other commercial enterprise ever has. Proudly proclaimed as the nation's smallest one hundred percent dieselized railroad, anything was permitted when visiting officials from Gardiner wanted to toy with their real live railroad. A caboose was dolled up, fancy toilet and all, and named "Perry's Pride" as a joke on company treasurer, Henry Perry. The railroad's annual reports, issued by President

Richard Greenwood, were tongue-in-cheek masterpieces of proclaiming what he deemed to be the shortcomings of the Internal Revenue Service and the Washington administration in general. They are now a collector's item.

For eight and a half years all went fairly well, if one can ignore the figures in red, but in November of 1957 there came the dreaded cry that Sykes had heard only once— FIRE! Although only part of the buildings burned, it was the death blow for both the industry and the nation's happiest little railroad.

William L. Sykes and associates have left their mark. More than one billion board feet of hardwood passed through their saws, most of it prime timber. There is no doubt that a good quantity of this still graces the bedrooms and living rooms of homes throughout the nation. But as with all mortal men, the hardwood king is gone and so is his Emporium, and its railroads.

The efficient little diesel locomotive that Heywood-Wakefield put into service on the Grasse River Railroad, photographed on the short run from Childwold to Conifer with engineer Larry Nicklaw. This picture has captured the complete motive roster of what was proclaimed to be the nation's smallest one hundred percent dieselized railroad. (*Photo by Paul S. Davis*)

Conductor Bill Tarbox waves from "Perry's Pride."

Cover and "Letter from the President," from the Grasse River Railroad 1957 Annual Report.

GRASSE RIVER RAILROAD CORPORATION
GENERAL OFFICES, CONIFER, N. Y.

The President's Letter

To the Stockholders:

About six months late, but not as late as we would have liked under the circumstances, I respectfully submit the Annual Report of your Railroad for 1957. Our attempts to forego the expense and trouble of telling stockholders that their Railroad floundered in financial quicksand for the 9th straight year was thwarted by a few over-zealous stockholders who stubbornly continue to associate railroading with profit. Our past experiences certainly should not have given them any such impression!

In the light of panic, shock and disillusionment in many business circles because of the continued slow-down of orders for goods and services, it must be comforting to stockholders to note that the Grasse River officers and directors are calm, cool, collected and unconcerned. Our experience with a business that consistently loses money year after year enables us to judge present conditions objectively and to check off the 1957 accomplishment as just another fly in the ointment.

We massed a perfect score of zero for incoming carloads in 1957. This contrasts with 6 the year before and 32 in 1955. Outgoing carloads, which are always more important, were 461 in 1957 as against 594 in 1956. We cannot explain this but you will be relieved to know that an employee more loyal to management is now doing the tabulation of incoming and outgoing cars. It is much easier to get new men from time to time to count carloads than increase the actual volume.

A quick review will reveal that the overall revenue decreased 31% with an operating expense decrease of only 7%, bringing about a decrease in net income of 68%. The important symbols in this gobbledygook are the percent signs. Or to say it in the vernacular, something went haywire again.

The greatest achievement of the year was the reduced contribution to the Department of Internal Revenue. For the third successive year we have continued to trim down our contribution toward keeping government bureaucrats "gainfully" employed. Our taxes dropped from $7,340 in 1955 to $7,182 in 1956 . . . and down to a handsome $2,295 last year. Such a tax gain ought to compensate for anything else that happened last year!

Every professional annual report should mention earnings. We have just mentioned them which should classify this report as official and in keeping with accepted accounting practices.

The downward "ski-jump" pattern of operations, illustrated on the front cover of this report, should be apparent at a glance. In no instance, during 1957, has any figure gone up. Total revenues, operating expenses, Federal income tax, operation ratio, net income, earnings per share and deficit per share have dropped to new lows. Some of these lower figures work to our advantage; others, like earnings and dividends, are sufficiently unimportant to have any true significance.

The elaborate and costly efforts made in 1955 in re-conditioning our passenger seating facilities (at the request of the ICC) have paid off handsomely. Passenger revenue in 1955 was at a new low. After the coach seats were cleaned and repaired, the 1956 revenue increased almost 4 times. And in 1957, passenger revenue went up another 33⅓%! Translating these complicated percentages into dollars and cents, the 1955 passenger traffic income was 60¢; in 1956, it was $1.50 (excluding a conscience contribution of $1.00 from Canada) and in 1957, paying passengers dropped $2.00 into the coin box! Such an experience with passenger traffic makes us wonder, quite frankly, why other railroads cannot increase passenger revenue as the Grasse River Railroad has done so consistently for three years.

Our experience in operating your property in a progressively declining pattern steels us against such newspaper headlines like: "President Asks Congress to Help Railroads." To railroad men inexperienced in unprofitable year-end results, such headlines ignite, perhaps, a spark of hope. We at Grasse River, however, already know how to lose money regularly without getting into astronomical figures that resemble the national debt or the unbalanced budget.

Nor have the rumbles about mergers caused us to perk up our ears to television antennae proportions. In all fairness to the many stockholders with huge investments in this link in America's vast transportation network, it must be reported that we have not been approached by adjacent railroads regarding our possible interest in a merger. Should such a proposition present itself, your capable management will exercise all of its many "horse-trading" skills, many of which haven't been practiced for years.

There is no substitute for good management except, perhaps, an inexhaustible supply of money. With no printing plants or U. S. Mints located on our right of way, we have had to rely wholly on railroading know-how and a fair share of luck. In both these categories we look for considerable improvement. In the meantime, your management is leaving no stone unturned in its efforts to give you the same kind of progressive, efficient and cool-headed leadership that has long showered your Railroad with managerial distinction.

Richard N. Townsend
President

Locomotive Roster: Emporium Lumber Company, Emporium Forestry Company, Grasse River Railroad

ENGINES LISTED IN ORDER OF PURCHASE

Orig. No.	Renum-bered	Builder	Builder's No.	Year Built	Type	Weight (tons)	Cyl. and Drivers	Source	Disposition
1		Homemade "Barney"		1885	Geared (3' gauge)		8 Drivers	Used at Benzinger	Sold 1897 Scrapped 1900
2		Homemade "Clyde"		1887	Geared		8 Drivers	Used at K.S. 1906 – Danby, Vt.	Scrapped 1950 at Conifer
3	33	Baldwin	6264	1882	0-6-0 ST	38	16" x 22" —38"	1900 – Miles Co. Used at K.S., 1913 – Conifer	St. Regis Co. in 1926
4	34	Shay-Lima	235	1889	2 Truck	15	11" x 10" —29"	Bought 1905 from C.H. & W.A. Rexford. Used at Galeton. 1912 – Conifer	Scrapped 1934 at Conifer
5	35	Climax	560	1905	2 Truck	60		New – 1905. Used at K.S. & Hammersley. 1912 – Conifer	1945 – Dexter Sulphate Pulp & Paper Co., Dexter, N.Y. Scrapped 1950
6	36	Climax	810	1907	2 Truck	50		New. Used Galeton & K.S.	Coal company in Pittsburgh
7	37	Shay-Lima	756	1903	2 Truck	70	12" x 12" —32"	From Campbell & Hagenbuck, Used at Galeton. 1917– Conifer	Dexter & Northern RR Scrapped 1943
8	38	Baldwin	12599	1892	0-4-4 T Forney	20	14" x 16" —42"	Elevated engine from Chicago & South Side. Used at Galeton. 1915 – Conifer	1923 – Tupper Lake Chem. Co.
9	39	Shay-Lima	1548	1905	3 Truck		12" x 15" —36"	1910 – Chapman Iron Coal & Coke Co. Used at Galeton. 1917 – Conifer	1929 – Glenfield & Western RR. Scrapped 1934
10	40	Shay-Lima	687	1902	3 Truck (Co.'s largest and best Shay)	92	14¼" x 12" —36"	1910 – Lackawanna Lbr. Co. Used at Galeton. 1917 – Conifer	1950 – Hey.-Wakefield Co.– 1950 Elk River Coal & Lbr. Co., W. Va. Scrapped 1962
31		Dickson	617	1888	0-4-0 ST		9" x 12" —29"	Bought 1910 from Lackawanna Lbr. Co. Used at Galeton	1918 – To Caflisch Lumber Co.
41		Baldwin			2-8-0 Fantail consolidated			Bought 1910 from E.H. Wilson & Co. Used at Austin	Scrapped at Galeton
42		Brooks	999	1883	0-6-0		17" x 24" —48"	Bought 1911 from BR&PRR To Conifer	1918 to Pittsburgh steel mill
43		Brooks	946	1883	0-6-0		17" x 24" -48"	Bought 1911 from BR&PRR To Conifer	1918 to Pittsburgh steel mill

Numbering series renumbered to 30s and 40s while in Pennsylvania.

Orig. No.	Builder	Builder's No.	Year Built	Type	Weight (tons)	Cyl. and Drivers	Source	Disposition
60	Schenectady	3902	1892	2-6-0 Mogul	60	19" x 24" —64"	1919 from NYC	Scrapped 1950 at Conifer
63	Schenectady	4553	1897	4-6-0	70	20" x 26" —57"	1923 – Potato Creek RR Used at K.S.	
61	Schenectady	3897	1892	2-6-0	60	19" x 24" —64"	ex NYC, 1923 from Rochester Iron & Metal Co.	1926 – Hudson Ship Bldg. & Repair Co.
68	Schenectady	3910	1892	2-6-0	60	19" x 24" —64"	1923 – Pa. Wood & Iron Co.	1949 – to Heywood-Wakefield Co. Scrapped 1951 at Conifer
71	Schenectady	3913	1892	2-6-0		19" x 24" —64"	1923 – Pa. Wood & Iron Co.	Scrapped 1949 at Conifer
3	Baldwin	13026	1892	0-4-4 T Forney			Midtolkian Country Club. Converted to gasoline power. Little used	Scrapped.
44	Climax	948	1909	2 Truck	30		1927 from Mt. Hope Coal & Coke Co.	1944 – Dexter Sulphite Pulp & Paper Co. 1948 – South NY RR Scrapped 1956
51	Shay-Lima	2758	1914	3 Truck		12" x 15" —36"	Jerseyfield Lbr. Co. No. 1 Bought 1930.	1948 – to Heywood-Wakefield Co. Scrapped 1950 at Conifer
52	Shay-Lima	974	1905	3 Truck	90	14" x 12" —35"	Jerseyfield Lbr. Co. No. 2 Bought 1930. Never used	Scrapped 1951 at Conifer
81	Shay-Lima	2881	1916	2 Truck		12" x 12" —36"	1934 – Basic Refractories Co. Never used.	Scrapped 1942
82	Shay-Lima	2755	1914	2 Truck		11" x 12" —32"	1934 – Basic Refractories Co. Never used.	Scrapped 1942
2	Alco-Schenectady	53845	1913	2-6-0 Mogul			Bought 1941. Mac-a-Mac Corp. No. 2	1949 – To Heywood-Wakefield Co. Scrapped 1951 at Conifer
1	GE-Erie	30783	1950	B-B Diesel 380 HP	44		Bought new by Heywood-Wakefield Co. (Not owned by Emporium)	1959 – EB&LRR

Total of 26 Locomotives — Homemade (geared), 2; Climax, 3; Shay, 8; Rod Engines, 13.

No.	Description	Source	Disposition
—	Evans Rail bus	Arlington & Fairfax	
1	"Will Roll Some" - Built from old Pullman car. Powered by 100 HP Sterling engine. Engine built 1906 – C/N 208002. 8-cycle – 100 HP	Built by Roy Sykes	
2	"Rolliam" - Converted from 1905 "Thomas Flyer." 4-cycle —50 HP	Built 1916 by Roy Sykes	
4	Motorized track car. Converted Baldwin No. 3, removed boiler powered with Sterling gasoline engine.	Shop built	Scrapped
11	"Jumping Goose" - Converted from 1931 White bus.	Built by Roy Sykes	1956 – Rail City Museum, Sandy Point, N.Y.
12	Rail interurban car	ex-Lancaster, Oxford & Southern RR, Lancaster, Pa.	1961 – Strasburg RR, Strasburg, Pa.

SCHEDULE
GRASSE RIVER RAILROAD CORPORATION
Eastern Standard Time
TIME TABLE No. 25 Subject To Change Without Notice **Effective 12:01 A. M., June 25, 1922**

	West Bound—Read Down				Daily Except Sunday		East Bound—Read UP			
	10	8	6	2		1	5	7	9	
	P.M.	P.M.	P.M.	A.M.		A.M.	P.M.	P.M.	P.M.	
....	8.38	5.10	1.10	6.40	Lv.......Childwold.......Ar	6.30	12.50	4.55	8.25	....
....	8.48	5.20	1.20	6.50	Ar.......Conifer.......Lv	6.20	12.40	4.45	8.15	....
....		5.25		7.20	Lv.......Conifer.......Ar		11.50		7.50	....
....		5.35		7.30	F....Grasse River Club....		11.40		7.40	....
....					F......Silver Brook Jct.					....
....		5.50		7.45	F.......Shurtleff's		11.25		7.25	....
....		6.00		7.55	F.......Clark's		11.15		7.15	....
....		6.15		8.10	Ar Cranberry Lake Lv		11.00		7.00	....
		P.M.		A.M.	F. Flag Stop for All Trains	A.M.	A.M.		P.M.	

ROY O. SYKES, Superintendent.

4

The "Peg-Leg" Railroad

by Richard F. Palmer

For years, the only way into the Fulton Chain of Lakes district of the Adirondacks from the "outside" was via the narrow, dirt, rough and tumble Brown's Tract Road from Port Leyden or Boonville.

The worst part of the ride was the buckboard trip through the woods from the Moose River Settlement in Lewis County to Old Forge in Herkimer County. But with the large influx of adventurers, tourists, and others after the "discovery" of the Adirondacks in the 1880s, it became increasingly apparent that a more congenial means of public transportation was needed. The only satisfactory answer at the time was a railway.

Four men were interested enough to plan and charter such a route, and they named the project, "The Fulton Chain Railroad." These men were Dr. Alexander H. Crosby, Samuel F. Garman, G. H. P. Gould, and Joseph A. Harvey, the latter the "tenant" of the Forge House in Old Forge village. All the men were partners in an area of land known as the Forge Tract.

Gould, at the time, also owned large timber holdings in the north branch of the Moose River valley, but it is believed that the three-foot-gauge railroad was not origi-

nally intended as a way of hauling logs. When it was first announced, in May 1888, that the line was to be built between Moose River Settlement and Old Forge, the De-Camp family expressed displeasure with the project on the grounds that a steam locomotive could set the woods on fire, although the *Boonville Herald* plainly stated, on May 3, that the road would be a "horse railway."

But Gould, who seems to have been the guiding light in the organization, decided against the use of horses and sent an order to the firm of Ryther & Pringle of Carthage, New York, for an inexpensive "homemade" locomotive.

That firm, in turn, ordered a boiler from the Ames Iron Works in Oswego, New York. The design was simple — there was to be only one piston and it was to be directly under the boiler. Gould also placed an order with the Carthage firm for an open-sided passenger car twenty-five feet in length and capable of seating twenty-five persons.

One end of the coach was to be sealed from the floor to the roof to act as a bulkhead to prevent sparks and rain from beating in on the riders. Meanwhile, he also instructed the builders to construct a small boxcar with doors in the center of each side for carrying luggage and

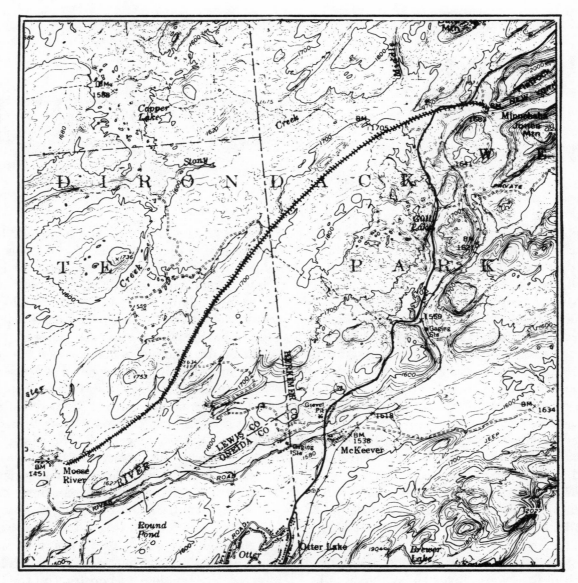

The "Peg-Leg" Railroad was so much a part of the woods it penetrated that even its rails were split from logs.

freight. Both cars rode on four-wheeled trucks at each end of the frames.

Work on the railway began in June, and a steam traction engine was used to saw the timbers which were used as track. At the same time, Gould had a small shed built at Moose River Settlement to accommodate the passengers' horses and buckboards.

The line was constructed by felling the straightest spruce and hemlock trees which could be found in the adjacent forests, and hewing them down from one end to the other for use as stringers. When laid on level ground the timbers were placed directly on the earth, but where the surface was uneven, they were seated on blocks of hardwood, or "shims."

Lengthwise, on the top of these heavy timbers, sawed stringers were spiked and the wooden rails were secured. No strap iron was used to cap the rails to prevent the wheels from crushing the wood. There is no evidence to show why this method of rail construction was employed, but it can be surmised that it was probably the cheapest and most expedient method.

During the early days of building, no cuts or fills were made, the track simply followed the natural contour of the ground. The right-of-way was accomplished by cutting all the trees which stood in the way.

Due to the primitive construction of the backwoods line, it is now thought that the wooden railroad might have been intended as a temporary measure, inasmuch as the Mohawk & Malone Railroad was about to start building its road only a few miles to the east, through Otter Lake, McKeever, and present-day Thendara.

By July 19, 1888, five miles of the railroad had been constructed and a steam locomotive had arrived, in pieces, by wagon, at Moose River Settlement. By late August it was assembled and placed on the new track, ready for its trial run. This proved to be a very unsatisfactory and disappointing event. When steam was applied to the single cylinder, the machine moved off gallantly, but after proceeding only one hundred feet it broke down and was unable to proceed. When repaired, it puffed up and down the completed portion of the track as a work train, carrying supplies and laborers to and from the advancing railhead.

But it was a frail machine and suffered numerous breakdowns. Many claimed that the crudely constructed track was at fault. Gould apparently realized that there had to be a more substantial piece of motive power and so went to a recognized manufacturer of locomotives for another engine.

He contacted the H. K. Porter Company of Wilkes-Barre, Pennsylvania, and after going over catalogs, he chose a saddle tank 0-4-2 with small 7"x12" cylinders (bore and stroke). Construction No. 1032 was given to Mr. Gould's new engine.

During the summer of 1888, a dam was erected across the north branch of the Moose River, thus making that body of water navigable to Old Forge.

Meanwhile, in September 1888, F. A. Barrett, proprietor of a stage line operating between Boonville and Old Forge, entered into an agreement with the Fulton Chain Railroad whereby passengers enroute would transfer at Moose River Settlement and continue their trip on the railroad. Before the line was completed, the backers of the project decided to terminate the track at the tiny hamlet of Minnehaha (also known to the local residents as Jones' Camp), four or five miles short of Old Forge.

During the following spring, a steamboat was constructed by William Scott DeCamp and dubbed the *Fawn*. Once launched, it began plying the miles between Minne-

The tiny train with its homemade cars awaiting the stagecoach from Boonville to transport passengers into the wilds of the Moose River country. (*Courtesy of Fynmore Studios*)

haha and Old Forge. The homemade craft was thirty-six feet long with two open decks and a paddlewheel on each side midship.

Steam to operate the paddlewheels was generated by an upright boiler located in the middle of the low hull and the stack extended about two feet above the roof of the open upper deck. As was typical of all riverboats, the craft sat extremely low in the water.

In April, before the winter snow had vanished, the new locomotive arrived at Port Leyden via the Rome, Watertown, & Ogdensburg Railroad. The thirty-six-inch-gauge machine arrived on a flatcar. It weighed eight tons, was equipped with a tight wooden cab, and carried its coal in a small fuel bunker on the rear of the engine frame. The water was carried in a tank that straddled the small boiler.

Port Leyden was located eleven miles southwest of the Moose River Settlement on the Black River. To get the engine to the southern terminus of the Fulton Chain Railroad was quite a task—but it was accomplished. Superintendent John McBeth and a gang of men used sections of track to do the job. The Porter 0-4-2 was steamed up and, after it passed onto one section, the section behind was moved around and put down ahead of the portion on which the engine stood. By repeating this procedure countless times, the engine arrived at Moose River Settlement under its own power. The journey had taken two days and two nights, May 10 and 11, 1889.

When the *Fawn* began operating in mid-June, the railroad owners and the DeCamps hoped that thousands of people would patronize their ventures. Both were an immediate success. The routes of the steamboat and the "Peg-Leg" railroad proved to be popular ones and the two stage lines were kept busy carrying passengers from Port Leyden and Boonville to Moose River Settlement.

After breakfasting at Charles Barrett's restaurant in Boonville, a traveler would board the stagecoach and start for Moose River Settlement. After a dinner of brook trout or venison, and fresh wild berries, the passenger would walk to the track of the short line railroad and board the open passenger car, the baggage being stowed away in the pint-sized boxcar.

At 1 P.M. the locomotive, with a full head of steam, would start forward, engineer W. H. Draper leaning out of the cab window to get the "high-ball" from McBeth. One rider wrote:

> . . . a car drawn by the iron horse within the shadow of the great wilderness, and (we) are soon plunging into its far-reaching depths. To say this is a narrow-gauge road, its curves gracefully abundant and its grades aspiring, and that the car is an open one except at the top and one end (a sufficient protection in this forest, where the rains descend perpendicularly, owing to the lack of wind), is to say the road is a unique work of rural mechanism conforming as far as possible to its surroundings; and hence highly conducive to the joys of romance and merriment of the journey.

The rough roadbed and sharp inclines did not permit much speed, but it was a pleasant eight-mile journey of two hours. The small engine was constantly sounding its little whistle to frighten the deer and bear from the wilderness right-of-way.

Upon arriving at Minnehaha on the north branch of the Moose River, the two-car train ground to a halt. A short spur led to the riverbank and the baggage was loaded onto a four-wheel track car for transfer to the steamboat, which was waiting at the dock.

Captain E. H. Sawyer was at the helm, while fireman Alonzo Crabb was kept busy in the tiny boiler room. The fare for the rail journey was a dollar, or about four and a half cents a mile.

The "Peg-Leg" operated only during the summer season, ceasing its runs early in October, after which time travelers were forced to return to riding buckboards.

During the winter of 1889-90, the company made improvements to its property. A depot, thirty by forty feet, was erected at Moose River Settlement, and the original route was changed in several locations to eliminate some of the steep grades and straighten some curves.

One local newspaper writer reported that "one road like this is worth a thousand buckboards," referring to the rugged Brown's Tract Road method of transportation.

During the course of the 1890 operations, the fear of the DeCamp family was realized when the locomotive did start fires in the adjacent woods. Fortunately, none proved serious and they were quickly extinguished by the train crew and "volunteers" from the ranks of the passengers.

When operations were resumed in the spring of 1891, Charles McMaster of Trenton, New York, was employed as locomotive engineer and James Cummings of Moose River Settlement, as fireman. McBeth resumed his position as ticket agent, telegraph operator, and train conductor. The "Peg-Leg" was the butt of many jokes, but despite the fun that was poked at it, its trains successfully managed to make daily runs with a minimum of trouble, and were well-patronized.

At times wet weather plagued the railroad in the summer months. Heavy and constant rains raised the level of many creeks, changing even many placid brooks into raging torrents. The Moose River rose up and flooded the lowlands.

At one time it was feared that the wooden track, along with its rolling stock, would be swept away downstream. The wooden superstructure was thoroughly saturated with water and the rails became extremely slippery.

The lightweight locomotive had difficulty, at times, in negotiating the slightest inclines on its daily trip. Invariably the engine would slip down and stall, the cabbage-cutter driving wheels spinning helplessly as the excess water was squeezed out of the damp wooden rails. McBeth would then ask the passengers to get out to lighten the load, and to help the train up the hill by pushing it to the summit of the small grade.

In August, for reasons now-unknown, both the engineer and the fireman quit their jobs. Instead of hiring a new crew, McBeth added these jobs to his already overburdened shoulders. The "Peg-Leg" was now truly a one-man operation.

As operations drew to a close in 1891, tragedy struck the railroad. At midnight on October 7, David Charbonneau discovered the tiny Moose River Settlement enginehouse engulfed in angry flames. He quickly gave the alarm, and McBeth successfully entered the shed and saved the company records. Damage to the Porter and the shed was estimated at $5,000, with no insurance.

The burning of the locomotive delayed the opening of the road to traffic in 1892, and it was late spring before the little engine was able to make its first trip of the season. On May 25 it set out from Moose River Settlement to Minnehaha. However, McBeth had taken departure from the company, having decided that running a saloon and boarding house at Nelson Lake was easier than running a backwoods railroad.

W. H. McGarry became the general freight and passenger agent and train conductor. Grant Bingham of Boonville was now the man at the end of the coal shovel.

The "Peg-Leg" was considered one of the wonders of the Adirondacks. This was because it was a scant eight

At Minnehaha, the steamboat, *Fawn,* on the way upriver to Old Forge. (*Courtesy of Fynmore Studios*)

miles long and constructed entirely of wooden timbers. The small steam engine, with its one-man crew, dragged the small train between the road's terminals, over the floor of the forest, and over ravines on stilt-like trestles twice a day. The one-way trip was made in less than two hours, depending on the circumstances. Many of the passengers were curious people who desired to see and ride this fabled primitive railroad.

Moose River Settlement was merely a jumping off place for supplies for the Mohawk & Malone Railroad, and by this time, the work on Dr. Seward Webb's new railroad was well underway. The "Peg-Leg" was exceedingly busy during the summer of 1892 hauling supplies for the new and larger railroad. While so engaged one day in June, the locomotive broke a side rod and jumped the track. Fortunately, the head end crew was able to jump clear and escape injury.

By July 1, 1892, the Mohawk and Malone had been completed to Thendara and the days of the "Peg-Leg" Railroad were nearing an end. The unique little woods railway failed to open the 1893 season. It became a fond memory and the forest reclaimed its own. The track rotted away, crumbling under the attack of weather and insects.

There was no further need for the log track meandering through the wilderness as passengers enroute to Old Forge and the Fulton Chain of Lakes could now ride the faster and more comfortable standard gauge line of Dr. Seward Webb.

Webb's trains didn't stall and ask the paid passengers to get out and push. Overnight the passenger car of the "Peg-Leg" was emptied almost instantly, and for the remainder of that last season it often ran without a single paying passenger aboard.

For many years hunters would stumble over the moss-covered remains, but with the passage of time only faint traces could be found by those who knew where to look. Today, it is next to impossible to find any signs of the "Peg-Leg," the long-gone Fulton Chain Railroad.

5

The Carthage & Copenhagen Railroad

by Richard F. Palmer

The quiet, old-fashioned north country village of Copenhagen regretted that the Utica & Black River Railroad had completely passed it by.

Although talk of constructing a railroad between Copenhagen and Carthage had been under consideration for some fifty years, no definite steps were taken until 1906.

By an almost superhuman effort on the part of the citizens of Copenhagen, the Carthage & Copenhagen Railroad Company was incorporated on April 2, 1906, with a capital stock of $100,000. James A. Outterson of Carthage was named president. On the board of directors were Addison L. Clark, John D. Wheeler, William J. Twining, John D. Dryden, Dwane G. Blodgett, and Frank P. Lansing, all of Copenhagen; and John E. Strickland, John G. Jones, Seth J. Gifford, and William B. Van Allen of Carthage.

Shortly after, on May 23, 1906, a contract for the construction of the 8.52-mile railroad was awarded to E. D. Bennett of Pulaski. Work commenced on the thirty-first of May and progressed rapidly that summer. By late summer the grading had been completed.

The tiny railroad's first locomotive arrived at West Carthage on October 7, 1906. It was an 0-4-4T purchased from the Mecca Lumber Company of Kalurah. This firm had purchased it from the New York Elevated Railroad and had used it for hauling logs out of the woods in the vicinity of Harrisville, a few miles east of Carthage.

So enthused were Copenhagen residents that the railroad was coming, they started talking of extending on to Oswego, but this never happened.

The C&C's first consignment of coal for Copenhagen arrived on December 28, 1906. It had to be left a mile outside of town because track laying had not yet been completed, due to difficulty in procuring an adequate supply of rails and ties. The locomotive developed the wheezes and had to be sent away to be repaired. Meanwhile, another engine was borrowed from the New York Central.

On February 18, 1907, eight carloads of produce were reported waiting to be shipped from Copenhagen, but had to wait awhile longer until the tracks were laid. A little wooden station was built at the foot of South Main Street in West Carthage.

In Copenhagen a barn was converted into a passenger station and freight house to serve as the terminal. In later

The pride of the Copenhagen Railroad was this trim little Mogul. (*Courtesy of Richard Palmer*)

years the women of the village raised enough money to erect a better passenger station which was used until the railroad was abandoned.

There was a "Y" at both terminals which permitted the locomotives to be turned. The coach, with "walk-over seats," was donated by Jimmy March, a former citizen who had won fame and success as a contractor in New York City. It came from the Erie Railroad.

Passenger service was inaugurated on March 12, 1907. The first train, consisting of the locomotive and the coach, left Copenhagen at 3:30 P.M. It was quite an event. But unfortunately, because of a lack of publicity, there was only a handful of people to welcome its arrival at Vrooman's Switch in West Carthage when the train arrived there forty minutes later.

The formal opening of the little railroad took place on June 28, 1907. Special trains were run all day on the eight-mile trip. Festivities included six trips over the line, a baseball game at which Copenhagen defeated Carthage 6 to 5, and a band concert at the Odd Fellows Opera House in Carthage.

That evening the opera house in Copenhagen was the scene of a formal banquet celebrating the railroad's birth. More than one hundred guests danced to Hungerford and Ryel's orchestra. The Rev. J. B. Felt of West Carthage was toastmaster. After a few selections by the Carthage Male Quartet, the train whistled out of West Carthage at 11:45 P.M. So with appropriate toasts, a few work cars, a second-hand coach, and an aging locomotive, a brave but almost hopeless transportation effort began.

The Carthage & Copenhagen was "everybody's railroad." The train could be stopped by a simple wave of a handkerchief. It picked up school children in the morning and returned them at night. It hauled the farmer's milk, cheese, cattle, coal, feed, and lumber. It did well for the first six months of operation but daily receipts soon fell to a meager handful as the novelty wore off.

The first timetable was issued on July 10, 1907. Trains were scheduled to leave Copenhagen at 7:50 A.M. and at 4:10 P.M.; and to return from Carthage at 9:50 A.M. and 6:30 P.M. each day. The trip took about a half-hour.

But the crew was notorious for not staying on the advertised schedule, especially during hunting season, when rifles and fishing poles often adorned the engine cab. It was truly a "Petticoat Junction"-type operation. Among the road's employees were Fred McIntyre and Charles Colegrove, engineers; Frank Barlow, superintendent; Alfred C. Stewart, general manager; Art Bigness and Al Clark, conductors; Frank Schramp, fireman; and Oliver Henry and Leslie Sheldon, agents at Carthage and Copenhagen, respectively.

For a time the freight business continued to grow, and the railroad purchased a 4-6-0 locomotive in September 1907, from the Jersey Central Railroad. A year or so later, No. 3, a 2-6-0, was purchased new from the Vulcan Locomotive Works. Another old teakettle, a 4-4-0, was also purchased, but it was soon sold to a contractor in Potsdam.

One of the most thrilling episodes in north country railroad history occurred on this line in the winter of 1914. Superintendent Frank Barlow said he was standing near two cars loaded with wood about two miles from West Carthage.

> As I stood near the cars which were connected to the rest of the train, which was on its way to Copenhagen, the cars suddenly pulled loose. I leaped on them just as they broke away and started their wild dash down the hill toward West Carthage. The grade was very steep and before the cars had gone far, they had gained considerable momentum.
>
> I was powerless to stop the cars. They crossed all switching and, after leaving our road, careened over the New York Central bridge across the Black River and headed for the local railroad yards. Villagers saw what was taking place and ran along to see what was going to happen.
>
> As the car I was on entered the yard, the milk train from Philadelphia, New York was just pulling in. Men saw that the two trains were about to crash, so they quickly shifted the cars onto a siding where several empty cars were standing. I was on top of one of them.

The Carthage & Copenhagen's McKeen railcar similar to the one pictured above which operated on the Ithaca-Auburn short line. These self-propelled cars, with their pointed cabs and porthole windows, were called "windsplitters." (*Courtesy of Richard Palmer*)

Just as they crashed, I jumped into the air and landed on the ground, not being injured in the least.

The influx of the automobile and motor truck became apparent after 1912 and business on the C&C began to wane. During World War I the company could barely meet the payroll. A bus service was soon begun on the state road between Watertown and Lowville, and the old coach was relegated to a siding and left to rot.

A spirited attempt to revive the railroad occurred on August 22, 1917, with the reorganization of the company as the Deer River Railroad. A short time later, the company purchased a second-hand McKeen railcar from the Buffalo, Rochester, and Pittsburgh Railroad. It was propelled by a 250-horsepower gasoline engine and was quite odd looking with its pointed nose and round windows. Built of steel, it was painted a bright red.

But all the efforts put forth proved futile. Charles E. Norris of Carthage was appointed receiver by order of the Supreme Court in November 1918, and the company was soon dissolved.

Operating expenses from January 1, to November 6, 1918 had been $26,760, while operating revenue was $19,269. Receipts for several years had been less than operating expenses, and the interest on $75,000 in bonds had not been paid.

For a time, trains were run only when there was enough for a full load. On January 8, 1920, the line was sold, for junk, to David Balmat, a director and general manager in its final years. The right-of-way was sold to Charles Pratt who used a portion of it for an electric power line that ran from a generating plant at High Falls on the Deer River, just east of Copenhagen, to Carthage.

After regular service had been abandoned, Brayton Austin of Carthage fitted an old touring car with flanged wheels and ran the mail and express to Copenhagen for a time. Locomotive No. 3 was sold to the DeGrasse Paper Company at Pyrites, in St. Lawrence County, and the other rolling stock was junked. The McKeen railcar went to the Narragansett Pier Railroad of Peacedale, Rhode Island.

The only remnant of this ill-fated venture in rural transportation is a half-hidden, weed-grown row of rotted ties, stretching off into the distance.

MOTIVE POWER ROSTER — CARTHAGE & COPENHAGEN (DEER RIVER) RAILROAD

No.	Builder	Bldr.'s No.	Yr. Built	Type	Cyl. & Drivers	Source	Disposition
1	Baldwin	4488	12/1878	0-4-4T	10" x 14" — 38"	ex-N.Y. Elevated RR No. 78, Manhattan Ry. No. 78; Sold 5/1903 to Mecca Lbr. Co. Kalurah, St. Law. Co. N.Y.; Sold 10/1906 to C&C	Retired 10/1908
2	Baldwin	2081	3/1870	4-6-0	18" x 22" — 56"	ex-Central RR of N.J. No. 268, renumbered to 812 in 5/1903. Sold to C&C 9/1907	
3	Vulcan	1252	10/1908	2-6-0	15" x 24" — 46"	Purchased new	Sold to contractor c. 1911 for construction project in Potsdam, N.Y., later scrapped
4	no data			4-4-0			
1001	McKeen	90	5/1910	rail car		Gasoline-powered. Ex-Buffalo, Rochester & Pittsburgh No. 1001; Sold 1917 to Deer River RR	Sold 1921, Narragansett Pier No. M-9; later scrapped

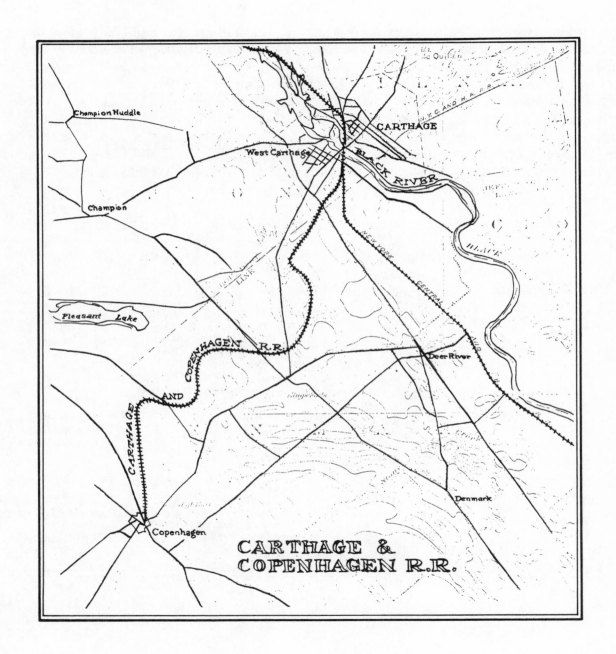

CARTHAGE & COPENHAGEN R.R.

110

6

The Adirondack & St. Lawrence Railroad

by Richard F. Palmer

The Adirondack & St. Lawrence undoubtedly was the only short line railroad built in New York State to transport "fool's gold!" Extensive deposits of ore had been discovered in the vicinity of DeKalb Junction, a few miles west of Canton, and in the 1890s, mining operations were begun by the St. Lawrence Pyrites Company.

Overnight a town called Stellaville sprang up to house the hundreds of workers employed in the mines. A mile-long rail spur was constructed to join the New York Central at DeKalb Junction and was eventually extended another two miles to the village of Hermon.

The Adirondack & St. Lawrence Railroad was incorporated as a common carrier in 1906 and passengers and general commodities were transported to supplement the transportation of ore.

The ore itself had a number of uses. Copper and alum, as well as sulphuric acid, were derivatives used in the manufacture of paper, pulp, and gun powder. Consequently, during World War I, the company found itself hauling a strategic commodity, and from January to June 1918 was under U. S. Railway Administration control.

Shortly after the war, the operation in Stellaville was closed down and the Public Service Commission granted permission to abandon the railroad. Stellaville became a ghost town. During the peak of activity, several hundred men had been employed in the mines and a large number of company buildings had been erected. For years the gaunt skeletons of empty houses, an abandoned mill, and piles of ore and tailings haunted the area. Gradually, what was left was carted away by scrappers.

The following story was written many years ago by H. F. Timmerman, the superintendent of the railroad. The account, accompanied by pictures, is courtesy of the St. Lawrence County Historical Association.

"Early in 1905 it was learned the Stella Mines located at DeKalb Junction and Hermon, New York, were to be reopened and operated with new management, under the name of St. Lawrence Pyrites Company. Pyrites is a type of iron commonly called "fool's gold." At that time I was employed by the New York Central Railroad as chief clerk in charge of accounts at DeKalb Junction.

Mr. Felix A. Vogel was general manager of the St. Lawrence Pyrites Company. He contacted me and outlined an

The Stellaville Mines, between DeKalb Junction and Hermon, were rich in deposits of pyrite, or "fool's gold." (*Courtesy of the St. Lawrence County Historical Society*)

idea the people of Hermon were promoting. They wanted the existing railroad from DeKalb Junction to the mines extended into Hermon. Before he committed himself he wanted to know if there would be traffic enough to warrant the extension.

He asked me if I would go over our records for the past three years and give him the amount of traffic to and from Hermon, Russell, and DeGrasse, to our station. I compiled this data and gave it to him.

Mr. L. A. Boyd, superintendent of the A&StL Railroad, asked me if I would meet him at DeKalb Junction. We rode locomotive No. 1 to the mines and walked over the right-of-way that had been obtained for the extension into Her-

mon. He told me that the road had been incorporated under the New York State Railroad Law, April 19, 1906, as a common carrier and included land purchased from Mr. Frank Glasby for yard sidings and a station. He planned to build the extension yard and sidings at Hermon, at DeKalb Junction, and at the mines in time to open the road for traffic on January 1, 1907.

He added another construction gang and wanted me to take charge. When this work was completed, I was to set up an accounting system for the railroad and the interchange with the Central, and also take the agency at Hermon. I accepted and obtained a leave from the New York Central and supervised building the extension and yards at Hermon. When Mr. Boyd completed the yard sidings at the junction, we consolidated both gangs to construct the sidings at the mines and mill. We worked ten hours per day, seven days per week. We had generally good weather, but during November and December we worked some rugged days and encountered some frost.

During the intervening time, the station at Hermon was completed and I had the accounting system set up. Because of the severe cold, Mr. Boyd, a southerner, resigned and returned to the south. Mr. Vogel appointed me acting superintendent, and before the road was formally opened, I became superintendent in charge of all departments, a position I retained until the road suspended operation.

In spite of the cold and snow, the last tie and rail were laid and the last spike driven (iron—not gold-plated), on Christmas Eve 1907. Before the road was formally opened, we ran several passenger trains out to DeKalb Junction and back, giving all who wished a free ride. We had a full load every trip. I think we carried more passengers that day than any day while the road was in operation.

Mr. Vogel felt like celebrating and invited everyone to a free dance to celebrate the completion of the road. He hired Mix's Hall and an orchestra. Mrs. Webb Mix kept the punch bowl well-filled and, apparently, the punch was plenty potent for everyone seemed to be in an exceptionally happy mood.

The road was formally opened for traffic on January 1, 1908, and we ran three round-trip passenger trains and one round-trip freight train a day. Our equipment consisted of Locomotive No. 1, a combination coach, ten box-cars, a flange car, twenty bottom-dump ore cars, and two side-dump tailing cars.

By the time we suspended operations years later, we had added another 66-foot combination coach and three more Baldwin-built locomotives. This additional motive power was necessary to take care of the increased business and to have one locomotive in reserve. To house them, we had to build another enginehouse. The traffic we were handling when the mines got going to full capacity and the other freight far exceeded our estimates, but due to the short haul, the rates we were permitted to charge were restricted by law. We were operating with a small net profit, but if faced with a costly accident or repair bill, our surplus would be wiped out. Our solution was to obtain more traffic and thus more revenue.

The surrounding territory was a heavy milk-producing area. This milk was manufactured into cheese, and several carloads were delivered to our station each week while the factories were operating. We knew if the milk was delivered to us in liquid form, our revenue would be many times greater, so we began to work on that angle. However, there were several factors to be considered: The supply of milk, a suitable location, a building, and a milk shipping company to sell the idea to.

The price fluid milk shippers were paying in other sections exceeded the price farmers received from cheese, and milk could be sold the year through, thus giving the farmer a steady income. We had a suitable location and building in the vacant wagon shop, situated on the west bank of Elm Creek, which would furnish ample supplies of water. This property was owned by James Brown and Louis J. Knox. I obtained an option on this property, went to New York City and interested the Mutual Milk and Cream Company in locating there. They sent men up to check into the matter. Later, they took up the option, installed the necessary equipment, contracted for a supply of milk, and started shipping fluid milk to New York City. This gave us a substantial increase in revenue.

Baldwin Moguls basking in the sunlight at the enginehouse near Hermon. (*Courtesy of the St. Lawrence County Historical Society*)

An early timetable is taken from the Official Railway Guide for December 1908.

Leave DeKalb Jct. for Stellaville and Hermon (4 miles)
‡9:35 A.M., *12 noon, ‡4:05 P.M., ‡7:20 P.M.
Returning, leave Hermon
*8:45 A.M., ‡10:00 A.M., ‡3:35 P.M., ‡6:40 P.M.
Running time, 15 minutes. Sept. 28, 1908.
Reference marks:
 * Daily; ‡ Daily except Sunday. Eastern time.
Connection with New York Central and Hudson River RR
 at DeKalb Jct.

Other traffic began to develop. Late in 1911 we leased land to R. J. Fairbanks & Sons, and early in 1912 they built a feed mill and coal silos. We built a track from our main line to their buildings. A Mr. Phillips leased some land on this track and built a maple syrup storage building. The Wayne Lumber Company purchased a large timber tract a few miles south of Hermon, built a mill, and shipped the lumber from Hermon station.

I contracted with Frank Angsbury, general manager of DeGrasse Paper Company, to furnish tailings from the St. Lawrence Pyrites Company mill to fill trestle approaches to the bridge spanning the Grasse River. Daily, for three months, we delivered three, 80,000-pound hopper-bottomed dump gondolas to the Central at DeKalb Junction, which they picked up and delivered to the paper company's siding at Eddy, east of DeKalb Junction. This was a good deal all around; St. Lawrence Pyrites saved the expense of drawing tailings to their dump; our road and the Central enjoyed substantial revenue; and the paper company got material for their fill at a lower cost than by any other method. Thus, our efforts to obtain more traffic began to pay off and our earnings improved.

More business was generated when Edward Burnam began a bus service between the town and the depot, which carried passengers and express, and when Thomas Hilton started his bus service from Russell carrying passengers, mail, and express. These new businesses not only benefited the railroad, but the town and surrounding area.

After operating a couple of years, Mutual Milk sold its business to the Northern Condensed Milk Company which enlarged the facilities, installed up-to-date condensing equipment, and contracted for a larger supply of milk.

When World War I broke out, they sold out to the Hires Condensed Milk Company, a subsidiary of Hires Root Beer. Hires increased the capacity of the plant and purchased several cheese factories, used them for receiving stations, and trucked their milk to the condensery. They also purchased a right-of-way for a spur track from our main line to their plant.

The Potsdam Stone Quarry, near Hannawa Falls, had suspended operation. We purchased steel rails from their tracks, took them up, and trucked them to the highway where Tim Snell picked them up and delivered them to the rail siding at Potsdam. We loaded them on flatcars and had them shipped to our yard at DeKalb Junction. That took care of the rail situation for the Hires spur.

However, ties were needed. We had only an emergency supply that could not be spared. I contacted the New York Central about the situation and they told me that they had a crew up in Quebec inspecting and loading ties. There were some that did not meet their specification, but would probably fill our need.

I went to Riviere du Loup, Quebec, and contacted a Mr. Crockett, the tie contractor. He took me up to his camp, a trip of twenty-three miles on the Timiscouata Railroad. I inspected, branded, and purchased ten carloads of cedar ties. When they arrived at DeKalb Junction, we built the Hires spur track which enabled us to shift carloads of coal, sugar, cans, and boxes to their plant.

After the United States entered World War I, Hires sold out to the Nestle Food Company. This firm enlarged and improved the plant and contracted for more milk. We handled one carload from Rensselaer Falls and one from Heuvelton every day.

We continued the successful and profitable operation until February 12, 1921. The St. Lawrence Pyrites Company had shut down after the Stellaville Mines were closed in January 1921. This, and the closing of the Nestles condensery, led to the decision to suspend operation of the railroad. All the rolling stock was sold. In 1924 and 1925 the tracks and bridges were removed and the corporation was dissolved on September 23, 1927.

Employees of the railroad included:

Wright Davidson, Claude Gates, Jay Rudd, Stanley Dygert, Glen French, and Henry Kenny, at the office and station; William Tull, Dan Clark, George Babcock, and George Whetmore, engineers; Charles Lephart, Edward Rerick, and Jay Rudd, conductors. Alton Foster was foreman of a section gang of seven to ten men; B. E. Jones was a joint agent of the NYCRR and the A&StL Railroad at DeKalb Junction."

Engine No. 2 siphons water into her thirsty boiler while the engineer takes a breather. (*Courtesy of the St. Lawrence County Historical Society*)

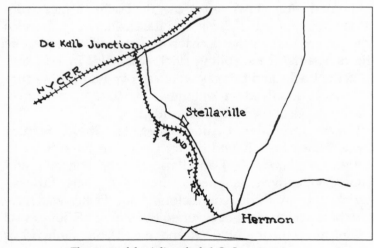

The route of the Adirondack & St. Lawrence.

LOCOMOTIVE ROSTER
ADIRONDACK & ST. LAWRENCE RAILROAD

1	2-4-0	no data			
2	2-6-0	Baldwin	C/N 33127	1/1909	18x24—48"
3	2-6-0	Baldwin	C/N 37400	12/1911	18x24—48"
4	2-6-0	Baldwin	C/N 14057	1894	

(No. 4 was originally built as Santa Fe No. 254. It was returned to the builder, and was resold to Toronto, Hamilton & Buffalo as their No. 22. Later it was sold to the General Equipment Co., who in turn sold it to the A&StL. It eventually was sold to DeGrasse Paper Co.)

7

The Crown Point Iron Company Railroad

by Richard S. Allen

Railroads have played a vital role in American history. Railroading today is on a huge scale, but less than a century ago there were hundreds of little ten, twenty, and thirty-mile railroads built not only to connect growing towns and villages, but also for industrial purposes.

One of the latter rail enterprises was the Crown Point Iron Company's Railroad. This was built and operated for the primary purpose of transporting the company's ore from the mines at Hammondville to the forges at Ironville, and to the furnaces on the shore of Lake Champlain at Crown Point. For twenty years it was also the winding, main artery of transportation up the valley of Puts Creek, connecting most of Crown Point's scattered settlements.

In 1873, Plattsburgh reporter, George F. Bixby, gave a running account of a trip aboard the CPI:

> Aboard we jump, the bell rings and away we go, with a long train of empty cars winding gracefully around the sharp curves. A mile up we stop a moment at the Crown Point Post Office to take on a case or two of goods, and then on goes the train up the valley of Putnam Creek, called "Puts" hereabouts. The engine, the "General Putnam," a coal burner, weight twenty-two

tons, pants and coughs as we toil up the crooked track which winds about the picturesque valley of the creek.

Onward and upward we go, for we must surmount the Kayaderosseras Range, Hammondville lying on the other side; the track continually cutting s's as it winds along the hillside. The engine labors heavily, the gauge indicating a pressure of one hundred thirty pounds of steam to the inch. Here, with a sharp turn, we glide over a trestle fifty feet high and then plunge into the dark green forest.

Two and a half miles up we pass the road leading to Crown Point Center, once a town of considerable importance, nestled among the mountains to the north. Three miles are passed, the grade becomes steeper. Here is a nearly level place; full steam is put on, and a tremendous rate of speed attained, but the acquired momentum is soon exhausted as we come to a sharp pitch. Another spurt and we reach the summit of Amy Hill, and as the train winds slowly around a curve, a most enchanting view of the valley below, with its villages, Lake Champlain beyond, and the green shores of Vermont on the other side, is obtained. We pass an old iron prospecting shaft and rush over Put's Creek on a long trestle. The valley now contracts more rapidly.

At Crown Point, the dual-gauge track system allowed compatibility between the narrow-gauge Crown Point Iron line and the standard gauge D&H.

The "General Putnam" takes on water at the "Old Furnace Tank." (*Courtesy of the Penfield Foundation*)

Onward we go until eight miles are passed when we come to Irondale, aptly named, owned by the company, and wearing the black, sooty look which is common to all iron manufacturing places. This is a small village lying at the north side of the track and you are at once struck with the air of neatness which its white cottages bear. All about, the hills are stripped of their timber far up towards their summit, and up by the margins of the forest, you see the old-fashioned charcoal pits smoking.

At Irondale we stop long enough to back the empty train up to a sandbank, where a portion of it is left. We pass a meadow and trout brook through which a heavy cut through the solid gneiss rock has been blasted. High rocky bluffs rise to the left and we are up above the old charcoal blast furnace. Panting, "General Putnam" stops here to take on water and we gaze about on the roughest, ruggedest, and rockiest of scenes. After a drink we trundle merrily on, at the summit of the grade now. An-

A picturesque scene along Crown Point Iron Company's Railroad run in 1874.

The "General Putnam" creaks across a high wooden trestle, 1874. (*Stoddard photo*)

other trestle and a nearer hill shuts off the bare precipice of Knob Mountain for a time. As we sweep around a huge curve, Paradox Lake and the distant valley of the Schroon River come into view. Just beyond, the landscape is tumbled into all manners of rough shapes. This is Hammondville, where the great Crown Point mines are located.

On the ride back, Reporter Bixby, a sporting man, elected to sit on the locomotive's cowcatcher. As can well be imagined, he was treated to a thirteen-mile downhill trip that rivaled anything Coney Island could offer.

Why was a railroad built up this valley? Iron was the reason from start to finish, and anything else was decidedly secondary. Beginning in 1826, the Penfield, Taft, Harwood, and Hammond family interests worked the iron deposits of Crown Point for over forty years. The Hammond blast furnace, in the notch of Knob Pond Brook, turned out top quality pig iron beginning in 1845. This was laboriously hauled by wagon to the lake at Crown Point, and then sent by canalboat to destinations such as Troy, Albany, Philadelphia, and Pittsburgh. Billets of wrought iron from the Penfield Forge in Ironville followed a similar journey to manufacturers.

The fine, pure quality of Crown Point Iron had always been well-known, but after the Civil War it came into further prominence. Samples were sent to England and used in making steel by the new air-blown Bessemer process. English experts pronounced the iron pigs from Crown Point the best to be found. The iron-makers of Albany and Troy who held the Bessemer steelmaking patent rights for America, considered the Crown Point deposits their major source of supply.

The town stirred and then became excited about the opportunities within its grasp. Crown Point's leading citizen, Civil War general, John Hammond, spearheaded the drive to expand the local iron business. In addition to the Bessemer steel men, the directors of the Delaware & Hudson Canal Company clearly foresaw Crown Point iron as a potential source of revenue. They planned to extend their railroad north from Whitehall along the shore of Lake Champlain to Canada, tapping industrial potential along the way.

Iron and lumber would be transported by rail from the north, while coal and manufactured goods would be shipped form Pennsylvania and the south.

President Thomas Dickson, of the D&H, foresaw these opportunities very clearly, and his company and business

A gully just out of Hammondville was bridged by this trestle. The bridgework on the Crown Point Railroad was a carpenter's dream.

associates invested heavily with the Hammond family of Crown Point to form a new and enlarged Crown Point Iron Company in 1872. This firm, under the direction of Gen. John Hammond, proceeded to consolidate all the local iron interests and activities. They purchased the old Hammond and Penfield ore beds on the mountain, and the original Crown Point Iron Company's blast furnace from which pig iron had gone to help build the famous ironclad *Monitor* of Civil War fame. At Irondale, or Iron-

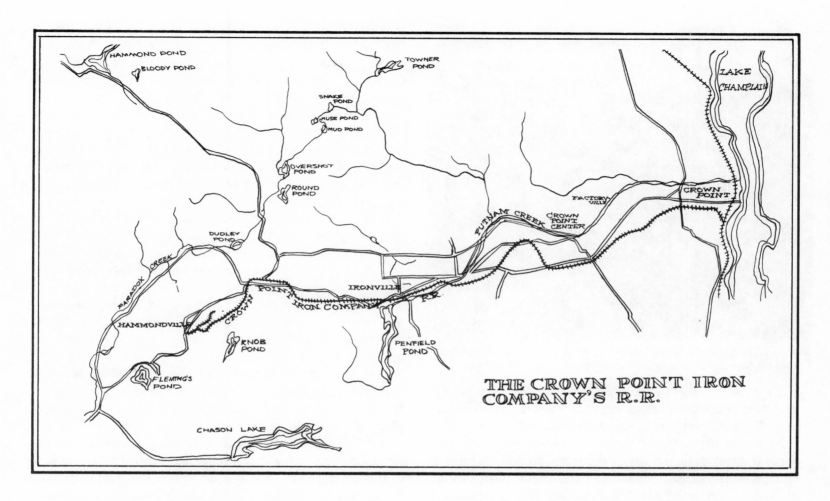

The following are labels on the map:

HAMMOND POND

BLOODY POND

TOWNER POND

SNAKE POND

MUSE POND

MUD POND

OVERSHOT POND

ROUND POND

LAKE CHAMPLAIN

CROWN POINT

FACTORY VILLE

PUTNAM CREEK

CROWN POINT CENTER

DUDLEY POND

PARADOX CREEK

IRONVILLE

CROWN POINT IRON COMPANY'S R.R.

HAMMONDVILLE

KNOB POND

PENFIELD POND

FLEMING'S POND

CHASON LAKE

THE CROWN POINT IRON COMPANY'S R.R.

ville, Allen Penfield and his son-in-law, Allen P. Harwood, sold out all their holdings: an iron forge, separator, water rights, saw and grist mills. At Lake Champlain the Hammond wharf property became the proposed site of not one, but two huge modern steam-operated, steel-jacketed anthracite blast furnaces. Surveys made at the mines showed new and even richer veins to be worked.

And with the top grade ore that would fill the maws of the Bessemer steel mills in Troy and elsewhere, Crown Point appeared to have a very rosy future.

To connect all the iron properties, separated by thirteen hilly miles and a 1,300-foot drop in elevation, a private industrial railroad was chosen. Though used as a common carrier, the line was always to be an important and inte-

This Stoddard photo shows the "diamond" where the Crown Point Railroad crossed the New York & Canada (later the Delaware & Hudson) Railroad.

The Civil War produced many picturesque and forceful men, among them another general, Alexander S. Diven of Elmira. A corporate lawyer, Diven was also a successful railroad contractor, and did much work for his friend Thomas Dickson of the Delaware & Hudson. The two men made a personal visit to the Crown Point properties on a hot summer's day in 1872. The stern, bearded visages of the railroad executive and the general were observed roaming the slopes of Put's Creek Valley, well-armed with liquid refreshment.

Dickson soon sent the D&H's chief engineer, Charles W. Wentz, up to Crown Point to survey the proposed railroad's route in detail. Wentz, a handsome man with fluffy sidewhiskers, worked his way over the hills with an eye glued to a surveyor's level.

During the winter of 1872-73, his assistants, tramping the frozen ground and snowy woods, ran out chain lengths and pounded stakes where the line would be built.

The route chosen began at the Whitehall & Plattsburgh Railroad tracks (later New York & Canada, then Delaware & Hudson), near the Hammond wharf at Lake Champlain. It curved around the north slope of Sugar Hill and crossed the Vineyard Road just south of Renne's, or Ranney's Corners. Always gradually ascending, it next looped to the north around the hill on which the Buck Mansion stood, and then crossed Put's Creek between Buck Hollow and Ironville. Swinging close to Penfield's Forge and the dam at Penfield Pond, the line was routed behind the church and parsonage at Ironville, and then across the road to the west. Closely paralleling the Old Furnace Road, the right-of-way was laid on up the mountain, with an extensive rock-cutting in the notch and along the side of the bluff just east of the old furnace itself. A high cross-

gral part of the iron company, and was officially termed, "The Crown Point Iron Company's Railroad."

From the first, D&H's Dickson took an extremely personal interest in the affairs of the iron company which he had made financially possible. A self-made businessman of Scottish extraction, he knew railroading, coal mining, and transportation; he also manufactured locomotives in Scranton, Pennsylvania.

On the local Crown Point scene, General Hammond took charge of the expansion and the building of the new facilities. He knew iron and iron manufacture in all its branches, but wisely put the building of the new little railroad in the hands of railroaders.

The "General Putnam" with its tiny train of ore-laden "jimmies," is shown at the Hammondville depot on October 7, 1874. The man standing on the platform with whiskers and cap is A. McDonald, Esq., superintendent of the Crown Point Iron Company. The man in white pants is Thomas Montague. "Big Knob" and "Little Knob" mountains are in the background.

ing at Knob Pond Brook brought the line into reach of the ore beds. Still another lofty traversal of a branch of Burnt Hill Brook took the rails into what would soon be the thriving community of Hammondville.

A partial list of Crown Point landowners whose property was purchased for a right-of-way contains many well-known names, among them Charles Hammond, Elmer Barker, Enos Bradford, Harry Dudley, James Taft, George Sisson, and Francis Wooster. Property ranged from almost eleven acres purchased from Helen Buck, who got paid first, to a little twenty-five by twenty-five-foot chunk on Sugar Hill belonging to a Mrs. Babcock.

In an effort toward economy and speed, something new was tried at Crown Point. This line was the second narrow-gauge railroad to be constructed in New York State. The first was the Central Valley, a five-mile line between Junction, about two miles south of Greene, New York, and Smithville Flats in Chenango County, built in 1872.

Crown Point's narrow-gauge followed by only two years the first of this type to be constructed in America, the 76-mile Denver & Rio Grande Line in Colorado. Standard gauge railroads, nearly all those in the United States, are 4'-8½" between the rails—a measurement that dates back to the width between the wheels of Roman chariots. Narrow-gauge is anything less than 4'-8½". The Crown Point Iron Company's Railroad was just three feet wide.

As with any railroad built during the financial crisis of the 1870s, costs had to be carefully considered. The advantages of narrow-gauge included less cost for rights-of-way and preparation, and cheaper, lighter rails, locomotives, and rolling stock. By following natural contours in hilly and mountainous country, the choice of the narrow-gauge could greatly reduce bridging, fills, and culverts. And, fortunately, Crown Point's terrain was ideally suited to this new type of railroad.

After a false start with a contractor who defaulted, General Diven's A. S. Diven & Co. was awarded the job of building the iron company's line in the summer of 1873.

General Diven's Irish laborers swarmed into Crown Point and made the dirt and rock fly. Foot by foot, section by section, the narrow-gauge took shape. The average cost per mile for the road was $26,000, a sizable sum to spend in a year of "tight money." It must be remembered that the railroad was only one portion of the gigantic iron-making and transport operation taking shape that year in Crown Point.

Norman Bly's sawmill on Put's Creek, below Crown Point village, supplied all the hemlock ties and the yellow pine timber for the eight trestles. That trestle over Put's Creek below Ironville consisted of a forty-foot Post Patent truss and heavy trestling which used 53,500 feet of pine lumber, making a structure 232 feet long. The trestle over Knob Pond Brook was a curved one, and the Miner's Trestle near Hammondville stretched 290 feet overall.

The forty-six-pound iron rails came from the Lackawanna Iron & Coal Company's works in Scranton, who in turn bought Crown Point iron with which to make more.

The line was uphill just about all the way, with a maximum grade of one hundred sixty feet to the mile, maintained for some ten miles. The steepest grade is reported to have been on the reverse curve just below Hammondville, where for one-fourth mile it was 168 feet to the mile.

Any operation other than mule-drawn work cars had to wait until the first new narrow-gauge locomotive could be built and delivered. The company ordered them from Thomas Dickson's Dickson Manufacturing Company. The first was outshopped in Scranton on July 24, 1873. With its delivery by railroad flatcar at Crown Point on August 19,

The "General Putnam" was later renamed "Hammondville," and by the mid-1890s, her traditional diamond stack had been replaced with a straight "capped" stack.

the CPI Company's railroad was in business.

Appropriately, this 22-ton, narrow-gauge locomotive was named the "General Hammond" in honor of the iron company's chief executive. Soon it was hauling work cars and workmen up the hill to the "end of track," a spot which gradually became further and further from the lake.

The "General Hammond," or as it was sometimes called, No. 1, commenced regular runs in January 1874, with newly-hired engineers on the payroll. A. S. Diven & Company completed their work of building the line shortly thereafter, and their shanties and shops became company property.

Though completed at Scranton in October, the second and third locomotives were not delivered until March 27, 1874. Duplicates of No. 1, they were the "Colonel Chitty" and the "General Putnam." The first was named in honor of Frederick Chitty, the then overall superintendent of construction for the iron company. The second commemorated the name of Revolutionary War general, Israel Putnam, who was associated with Crown Point in French and Indian War days, and for whom Put's Creek was affectionately named.

The great majority of the Crown Point Iron Company Railroad's rolling stock consisted of ore cars, most of which were built in the line's own machine shops at Crown Point. They were little four-wheel jobs, made of oak and lined with plate iron, with a center drop for unloading. They had a capacity of from five to six tons, and about a hundred of them were usually in daily service. It took nearly twenty ore cars to load an average-sized canal-boat.

With orders from the steel mills for amounts like 60,000 tons, the two "Generals" and the "Colonel" were kept busy shuttling ore cars back and forth between Ham-

mondville and Lake Champlain. Additionally, as much of the ore was processed in the separator at Ironville in order to yield a higher metal content, it had to be transported there as well. Ore and iron products made up to ninety-three percent of the railroad's shipments, year after year.

Other rolling stock on the CPI Company's Railroad consisted of a combination mail and passenger coach, two cabooses, three boxcars, six flatcars, and three tool cars. Strangely, though it operated during the winter, the company seems to have gotten along without a snowplow.

The up-hill and down-dale layout of the railroad made for comparatively easy work on the part of the locomotives. Depending on conditions in the fluctuating iron industry, they made at least two and sometimes four daily round trips. Snaking a string of empties up the thirteen miles of main track to the mines, they would return with the heaviest load their brakes could safely handle, using hardly any steam power. Much time was spent positioning cars on the spurs and sidings. These, when added to the main line's total, brought the road's track mileage to exactly twenty.

Passengers were, for the most part, company employees, carried in mixed trains at the average speed of twelve miles per hour. They were issued regular tickets, a number of which were put on display in the Penfield Homestead, and sold an average of about 8,000 a year. During the later years of operation there was little or no accounting of whether a rider paid or not.

Everything sent up the line was first unloaded from the standard gauge cars on the main line of the D&H, and then reloaded onto the narrow-gauge cars. Though a nuisance, it had to be tolerated. The flats and boxcars brought up supplies for the company stores at Ironville and Hammondville: groceries, produce, dry goods, hats, glassware and crockery, boots, shoes, kerosene, drugs, tools, black powder, and nitroglycerine.

At least two pianos came up to Hammondville during the first year of operation—one for Captain MacDonald, mines superintendent, and one for Professor Herring, the company's chemist. It would be interesting to know if the two men ever indulged in piano duets, with the strains of Mozart or Brahms floating on the mountain breezes.

The railroad also held the main contract to supply the Crown Point, Ironville, and Hammondville post offices. This added about $520 a year in revenue.

On October 7, 1874, the well-known Adirondack photographer, Seneca Ray Stoddard, paid a visit to Hammondville. With his portable darkroom mounted on a flatcar behind the trusty "General Putnam," Stoddard took photographs at strategic points along the railroad, recording the engine along with accompanying scenery and iron operations. To this visit we are indebted today for a priceless—though incomplete—series of photographs of the Crown Point Iron Company's Railroad, plus the Lake Champlain wharves, Ironville and Hammondville, as they appeared nearly a century ago.

The men who ran the railroad were well-trained, most of them machinists and tinkerers with native intelligence and curiosity, who worked their way into locomotive operation. Personnel ranged from twenty-five to as many as forty depending on the vicissitudes of the iron business. Among the locomotive engineers were Tom Griffiths, John Tallman, Jim West, John De Wolf, Emory Gokey, and W. H. Curtis. A. H. Barse spent at least eleven years in the right-hand seat of the company's locomotives. Engineers received $1.20 per day, only thirty cents less than the top pay generally reserved for the foremen in the company.

Cornelius Ryan was conductor for nearly all the twenty years of the railroad's existence, and he drew extra pay as janitor of the company's offices at Hammondville. Another conductor was George D. Gage. There was even one woman employee, Mary Ann Cahill, who briefly served the company at $4.00 a month as "watchwoman."

Only a few of the railroaders were of Irish extraction, though many Sons of Erin worked in the mines, along with French-Canadians, English, and a number of Scandinavian immigrants. The majority of railroad employees were natives of New York and nearby Vermont.

The Crown Point Line never had any spectacular accidents, such as engines plunging off the trestles or meeting head-on. One employee was killed in 1887 and another lost an arm in 1891, and there were a number of fatal accidents at the crossings, particularly in the mine area. But as far as can be ascertained, no passenger on the railroad was killed, or even injured.

In 1875, a fourth locomotive was added to the roster; a 27-ton saddle tanker from the Baldwin Locomotive Works in Philadelphia. Though built by a competitor, this engine was given the name "Thomas Dickson." In service with the Crown Point Iron's railroad for eighteen years, and held in storage another ten, the "Dickson" never went to Hammondville, or Ironville, or even to Sugar Hill. It couldn't, because it was standard gauge. The company used her to shuttle ore and freight cars about the furnace grounds at the lake and to do D&H switching on the sidings.

The last locomotive that came to Crown Point in 1883 was another narrow-gauge from the Dickson works in Scranton. This was a big 40-ton Mogul named "Crown Point"—nearly twice as heavy as the original engines. About this time the "General Hammond" and the "Colonel Chitty" disappeared from the roster, but the old "General Putnam," with an extended boiler and renamed

Seneca Ray Stoddard captured the spirit of railroading of the 1870s on the Crown Point Railroad, presumably at Hammondville.

"Hammondville," continued to labor on.

It is told that General Hammond once had a threatened strike on his hands at the mines. He sent word down to the lake, and a group of his fellow cavalrymen from Crown Point grabbed their rifles and scrambled aboard a locomotive. The trip up to Hammondville took just half an hour, the fastest time recorded for the journey. With armed reinforcements, the general speedily broke up the labor troubles.

A telegraph line was strung along the tracks in 1888. By that time Thomas Dickson had died, and Crown Point's John Hammond was forced to resign from the company he had done so much to found and develop.

Joint management with the Chateaugay Iron Company to the north gave decided preference to the use of Chateaugay ores. Before long, absentee ownership and operation let the property, and the railroad, deteriorate alarmingly. When competition with Minnesota's Mesabi and Lake Superior iron began in the 1890s, it was considered uneconomical to continue operation of the Hammondville mines, the Ironville forges, the Crown Point furnaces, and the Crown Point Iron Company's railroad.

The last shipments of ore came down the mountain to the furnaces on July 22, 1893, and to the separator at Ironville on July 31. Engineer John DeWolf, with W. H. Curtis firing, operated locomotives during August, apparently to collect stray cars along the line and to perform miscellaneous work. After that, everything came to a standstill and operations ceased. With the mortgage and sale of the entire property to American Steel & Wire, all structures were razed and the rails removed from the right-of-way.

The old saddle tanker, "Thomas Dickson," was briefly called back into service in 1903, during experimental work at the old blast furnaces by Lake Champlain. The two narrow-gauge locomotives were sold, and the ore cars and other rolling stock consigned to scrap.

There is a persistent rumor that, in the 1930s, the old "Hammondville" was seen doing duty on a coffee plantation in Brazil, but the chances of tracing down the truth of her final disposition grow slimmer and slimmer with each passing year.

Except for obliteration at the lower end of the line, the old roadbed of the CPI Co.'s Railroad is surprisingly intact for all of its thirteen miles and most of its sidings. It would be entirely feasible to restore many stretches of roadbed and track. The trestles have rotted away, but the rock cuttings and embankments will probably give an indication of the hand of man on the Crown Point landscape for a long time to come.

Even today it is readily possible to conjure up a mental picture of a Crown Point iron train coming down from the mines.

The Crown Point Iron Company's only standard gauge locomotive, "Thomas Dickson," is seen doing switching chores at the D&H interchange at Crown Point.

ROSTER OF CROWN POINT IRON COMPANY'S RAILROAD LOCOMOTIVES — 1873-93

No.	Name	Builder	Bldr's No.	Year Built	Type	Weight (tons)	Cyl. & Drivers	Disposition
1	Gen. Hammond	Dickson	126	7/1873	2-6-0 narrow-gauge		11" x16"—37"	Disposed of prior to 1885
2	Col. Chitty	Dickson	127	10/1873	2-6-0 narrow-gauge		11"x16"—37"	Disposed of prior to 1885
3	Gen. Putnam (later Hammondville) (In 1896 reported as "Mogul" with 36 wheels, Straight stack. Wt. 22½ tons - 55,000 lbs.)	Dickson	128	10/1873	2-6-0 narrow-gauge	22	11"x16"—37"	Disposed of after 1896
4	Thomas Dickson (In 1896 reported as saddle tank, straight stack, vacuum brakes. Wt. 27 tons – 58,000 lbs.)	Baldwin		1875	0-4-0 standard gauge	27	15"x22"—45"	Disposed of after 1903
5	Crown Point (Original name "Crown Point." Cost $8,000. In 1896 reported as "Mogul" with 36" wheels, straight stack, extension front, vacuum brakes. Wt. 45 tons – 91,000 lbs.)	Dickson	425	5/1883	2-6-0 narrow-gauge	45	15"x18"—36½"	Disposed of after 1896

The "General Putnam" on one of the many trestles on the Crown Point Iron Company's Railroad, against a backdrop of majestic Knob Mountain.

8

The Williamstown & Redfield Railroad

by Richard F. Palmer

In the 1860s, northern Oswego County, like other up-state New York areas, abounded in tall stands of beech, spruce, hard maple, and hemlock. Realizing the potential of the area as a source of lumber, Calvert Comstock entered into a contract with the New York Central Railroad to furnish timber for ties, buildings, and firewood.

The most economical means of getting this timber out of the woods was to build a railroad northward from the Rome, Watertown, and Ogdensburg Railroad at the village of Williamstown.

A line was constructed a few miles into the forest, and in no time a little village called Maple Hill sprang up. It was named for an area never breached by the iron horse.

At Maple Hill, several steam sawmills were built, one of which was capable of sawing eight million board feet of lumber a year. Two of the mills were operated by the Williamstown & Redfield Railroad and Forest Company and another by William Maher. At its peak, the company employed more than five hundred men in the woods and railroad operation. Some of the workmen lived in a boarding house operated by Brian Goode. The company operated a store where employees could buy their supplies.

And, in 1863, the Maple Hill post office was established and John H. Wardwell, a "general merchant," was named postmaster. About the same time, a schoolhouse was built.

By the end of the Civil War, about six or seven miles of railroad had been constructed. On March 31, 1865, the Articles of Association of the Williamstown & Redfield Railroad Company were filed with the Secretary of State in Albany. The capital stock was $200,000 in shares of $100 each. Old-time railroad magnates were by no means pessimistic. A clause in the fading document reads:

> This company shall continue for the term of 1,000 years. The undersigned hereby form a company for the purpose of maintaining and operating an unincorporated railroad already constructed for public use in the conveyance of persons and property and for the purpose of constructing, maintaining, and operating a railroad for like public use, including enlarging and extending the aforesaid unincorporated railroad constructed.

Directors were Mr. Comstock, Lewis Lawrence, Lewis H. Lawrence, Hiram Hurlburt, George Tallman, Enoch B. Armstrong, and Bloomfield J. Beach, all coming from the Utica-Rome area.

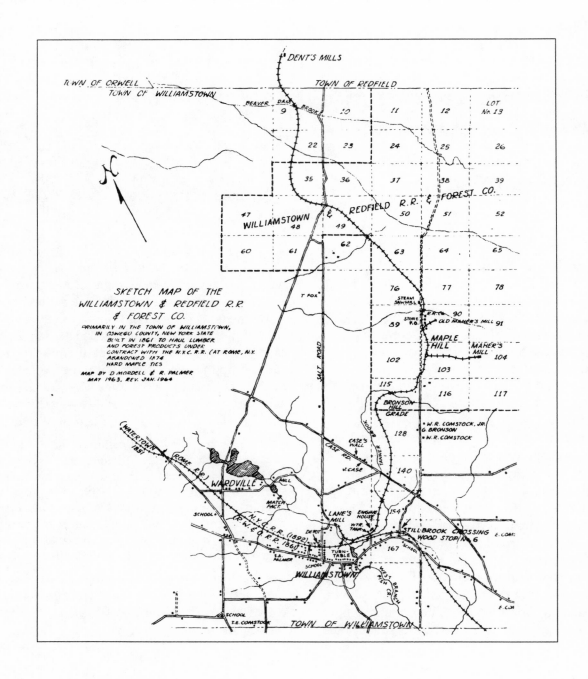

DENT'S MILLS

TOWN OF ORWELL
TOWN OF REDFIELD
TOWN OF WILLIAMSTOWN

BEAVER DAM

9   10   11   12   LOT No. 13

22   23   24   25   26

35   36   37   38   39

WILLIAMSTOWN & REDFIELD R.R. & FOREST CO.

47   48   49   50   51   52

60   61   62   63   64   65

76   77   78

SKETCH MAP OF THE
WILLIAMSTOWN & REDFIELD R.R.
& FOREST CO.

PRIMARILY IN THE TOWN OF WILLIAMSTOWN,
IN OSWEGO COUNTY, NEW YORK STATE
BUILT IN 1861 TO HAUL LUMBER
AND FOREST PRODUCTS UNDER
CONTRACT WITH THE N.Y.C. R.R. (AT ROME, N.Y.
ABANDONED 1874
HARD MAPLE TIES

MAP BY D. MORDELL & R. PALMER
MAY 1963, REV. JAN. 1964

T. FOX

STEAM SAWMILL

STORE P.O.   R.R. CO.   90
89   OLD MAHER'S MILL 91

MAPLE HILL   MAHER'S MILL
102   103   104

115   116   117

BRONSON HILL GRADE

CASE'S WALL

W.R. COMSTOCK, JR.
G. BRONSON
W.R. COMSTOCK

128

(WATERTOWN 1851

ROME R.R.)

CASE RD.

J. CASE

140

WARDVILLE

MILL

MATCH FACE

SCHOOL

LANE'S MILL   ENGINE HOUSE
WTR. TANK

154

N.Y.C. R.R. (1892)
R.W. & O. R.R. (1861)

DEPOT

STILLBROOK CROSSING
WOOD STOP No. 6   E. COM.

TURN TABLE

S.A. PALMER

SCHOOL

167   SCHOOL

WILLIAMSTOWN

WEST BRANCH FISH CR.

E. COM.

SCHOOL
T.B. COMSTOCK

TOWN OF WILLIAMSTOWN

E. COM.

SALT ROAD

TANNER ROAD

The promoters, it is said, had plans to extend the line to Redfield village (formerly called Centre Square). It was thought the town fathers would consent to putting a bridge across the Salmon River, but they never did.

Why? One theory is that the people of Redfield didn't want to risk losing mail-hauling contracts on the Sackets Harbor Post Road. Another is that they may have thought the railroad would continue on to Osceola which would have enjoyed the distinction of being called a railroad terminal.

Engineers on the rail line were Henry Greene and his two sons, Edward and William. Mr. Comstock had a home constructed for them adjacent to the enginehouse in Williamstown.

A few interesting anecdotes have somehow survived down through the years. One story is told of a farmer near Pekin, a hamlet south of Orwell, who was so eager to have the railroad pass his way that he built an enginehouse. When the railroad extension failed to materialize, he moved his belongings into it and lived there ever after. Legend has it that a pro-railroad faction in Redfield actually built a few hundred yards of grade and even a depot.

And then there's the story of blacksmith Dave Shaw's hair-raising experience in the cab of the "Maple Hill Railroad" locomotive.

One evening he was riding in from the woods, and as the engine rounded the curve into Williamstown, ". . . the firemen let out the darndest yell I've ever heard in my life. Just then we went slam, bang, smash, through three or four cars the RW&O boys had "shoved clear" onto our main track instead of leaving them back on the unused connection."

From the enginehouse, the lumber railroad swung to the northwest a few hundred yards to Lane's Mill, where logs were unloaded for sawing. The Comstock firm also furnished large quantities of bark for the famous Williamstown Tannery on Fish Creek, at one time reputed to be the largest in the state.

But all was not bread and honey in the old days. Life was hard. Youngsters were forced to seek work at an early age. One such person was James H. Kinney, who was born in Evans Mills in 1856 and died in Brewerton in 1929.

Mr. Kinney once related that his father was killed in the Civil War. His mother then took the family to the vicinity of Williamstown, as it was a growing community. But it was pretty rough going. She found meager employment doing odd jobs, such as washing and sewing. The children's clothes at times were made of old grain sacks. Everyone had to work.

"Jimmy" found a job at the tender age of twelve, driving a team hauling wood for the Williamstown and Redfield Railroad.

The railroad also had it share of accidents. Once, Tom Ryan, a brakeman, was seriously injured when a couple of cars loaded with shingle bolts got away on a grade and tore down the line to Williamstown. Aware of impending disaster, Ryan tried to burrow himself down into the wood rather than suffer the consequences of jumping off. When the train rounded Bronson Hill grade, it flew off the track and Tom went with it. One leg was so badly mangled it had to be amputated. After that episode Mr. Comstock insisted that at least three brakeman ride on a train.

In 1868, there were eight steam sawmills operating in the vicinity of Maple Hill. About 1870, the railroad was extended several miles northwesterly into the town of Redfield to a place called Dent's Mill, operated by Samuel Dent. That same year, the W&R Railroad and the mills connected with it operated year around, rain or shine. The three sawmills at Maple Hill alone employed more than two hundred men. The mills were equipped with burr saws powered by steam engines. According to the census the annual yield for hemlock and spruce was five million board feet. A year later the contract expired, but was renewed for two or three years.

Maple Hill ceased to have a post office in 1873. The 1875 census of Oswego County noted, "a large wood job had been partially stopped, reducing the population (of the town) to about one hundred forty persons." Some work was carried on until 1876, when the mills were dismantled and the railroad abandoned, as the best of the timber had been cut. The 1878 Oswego County History notes: "Several buildings that were constructed while this contract was in operation are still standing, but unoccupied."

It is interesting to note how communities flourished one day and vanished the next. Such was the plight of old-time lumber towns.

After the operation was abandoned, the Comstocks retained ownership of the properties, and left the rails in for several years. Neighborhood farmers were allowed to use the railroad to take out small quantities of wood on pushcars.

Finally, the lower bridge over Tanner Brook, near Williamstown, collapsed under the weight of a pushcar, and the Comstocks had the tracks removed, lest someone be injured and hold them liable.

Finally, on December 30, 1927, the Comstocks deeded the property to the Blount Lumber Company of Lacona, who logged it for a time and then sold it to a private individual. It was seized by the county of Oswego for failure to pay back taxes.

So died the Williamstown & Redfield Railroad, its days of usefulness ended. Today one can still find traces of the embankment, winding its way northward to a town that no longer exists. Brush and dense undergrowth hide traces of the old enginehouse at Williamstown.

At the former Case Road Crossing (named for Jerome I. Case, founder of the company of the same name, who lived nearby as a youth), there's a curious looking rectangular hole in the ground, lined with cut stone. It is said that it was a cattle guard. When an unwary bossy tried to reach greener pastures, she'd stumble into the pit, about three feet deep, which was filled with water. There she'd stay until someone came looking for her.

At the enginehouse, a little scratching reveals wood ashes where Engineer Greene dumped the fire of his Iron Horse so long ago.

Williamstown & Redfield Railroad.

No. 270

FREIGHT WAY-BILL

FROM

MAPLE HILL

TO

Williamstown

October 2 1871

9

The Marion River Carry Railroad

by Richard S. Allen
& Richard F. Palmer

The hunter had been lost for days. Wandering through the still forests of the Adirondack wilderness, he knew he couldn't last much longer. Floundering among the boulders of an icy river, he clawed his way up the far bank. In the darkness his outflung hand gripped a protruding timber. It wasn't round, but a hewn-out square. To the right was another, and another. The lost hunter poked up his rifle and gingerly tapped between the beams and was rewarded with the ringing clang of steel on steel.

"The only one in miles," he muttered. "It's the Carry Railroad."

Two hours later, the crew of the "Shortest Standard Gauge Railroad in the World" found him blissfully asleep beside the tracks, confident that he had reached safety.

By 1900, the vast north woods—New York State's Adirondack Mountains—was the mecca of thousands of fishermen, hunters, and holiday-minded seekers of healthful solitude. New York City dwellers, in particular, "discovered" the Adirondacks after the railroads had opened up this unspoiled wilderness.

Dr. Thomas C. Durant's Adirondack Railway (later absorbed by the Delaware & Hudson) was the pioneer in promoting north woods' travel. Opened to North Creek in 1871, the line became the jumping-off place for horse-drawn stage lines radiating into the mountain region. Wilderness guides set up primitive boarding houses for the summer visitors and led them to the shores of Indian, Long, and Blue Mountain Lakes.

Adirondack transportation was a challenge to builders who claimed steel rails could be laid just about anywhere. But the Adirondack Railway had fallen considerably short of its original goal by establishing a permanent railhead at North Creek—many miles short of what was to become the traditional resort areas.

Dr. Durant's son, lean, keen-eyed William West Durant, had no illusions of becoming the empire builder his father had been. The Adirondack Railway had been sold to the Delaware & Hudson for a reputed paltry $690,000. But he still retained vast land and timber holdings of wilderness, including the "Eckford Lakes"—Blue Mountain, Eagle, and Utowana.

Since Raquette, Utowana, Eagle, and Blue Mountain Lakes were all connected by the navigable Marion River, Durant established a line of small steamboats as the next logical link into the Adirondack wilderness.

But there was one small break in the thirteen-mile water route from the dock at Durant to the big hotels on Blue Mountain Lake. Emerging from Utowana Lake, the Marion River, for a short distance, become a turbulent, twisting, rock-strewn mountain torrent. Since Indian times, to overcome the twenty-seven-foot descent, there had been a portage there. Generations of Indians, trappers, and hunters had shouldered their canoes and guideboats up and down the 1,300-yard path between still waters. The place had long been called "Bassett's Carry," named for a woodsman whose cabin stood beside the hard-packed path. Later, the Carry Inn was built to cater to the needs of tired and hungry portagers.

Because of the carry, Durant had to have two sets of steamboats: one for Raquette Lake and the lower Marion River, and the other to ply the waters of the upper lakes. At first the portage was accomplished by means of wagons on a widened path. Passengers, baggage, mail, freight, and small boats were all jumbled together on a wagon. Originally looked upon as a lark by travelers, it soon became a nuisance.

But William West Durant was both resourceful and imaginative. After rejecting a plan to bypass the carry with a canal and locks, he concluded that a railroad would do a better job and a cheaper one. He directed his surveyor, Wesley Barnes, to plot out the best route.

Once decided upon, work on the railroad began during the summer of 1899 and was ready for operation in the spring of 1900. Roughly S-shaped, the line, with sixty-seven-pound (to the yard) rails, followed the north bank of the tumbling Marion River, swung across it at the foot of the old portage, and continued with a gentle descent to a new dock on a quiet reach of the river. The length was

138

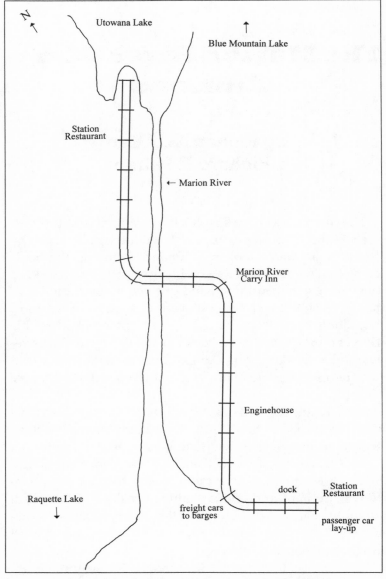

Map of the Marion River Carry from a sketch by Michael Kudish.

This very early view shows the original locomotive No. 1 and two cars, at the lower end of the Marion River Carry. The initials "F.P.&L. Co." on the engine and cars denote "Forest Park & Land Co." (*Courtesy of The Adirondack Museum*)

approximately seven-eighths of a mile. Although the claim that it was the "shortest standard gauge railroad in the world" might be debatable, the Marion River Carry Railroad was certainly one of the shortest to have its own motive power and rolling stock. The line cost ten thousand dollars to construct.

Durant, now laughingly referred to as "a pocket-sized railroad magnate," searched for rolling stock. On Long Island he found three small four-wheel cars which had been used on the original horsecar lines of the Brooklyn Rapid Transit Company. One was altered by removing the seats so it could be used for toting boats, baggage, and freight. The other two open cars, with seats facing in either direction, could seat forty passengers. Durant paid seventy-five

dollars for the three cars. Shipped to the Adirondacks and towed across Raquette Lake on a makeshift scow, they were put to work on the carry railroad where, for a time, they were pulled by horses just as they had been in Brooklyn.

The first steam locomotive on the carry line was a small, four-wheel "dummy" engine formerly used on the elevated railroad in New York City in the days before that line was electrified. Prior to its arrival in the Adirondacks, "No. 1" was converted to burn oil by shop crews at the Schenectady Locomotive Works.

On its arrival in May 1900, engineer W. H. Horton found that the balky kettle with an upright boiler lacked the power to haul the cars. By midsummer it was dis-

139

carded for a heavier switch engine leased from the New York Central for five dollars a day.

While No. 1 was too light, the leased locomotive was too heavy and was expensive to operate. Mr. Durant then ordered a new locomotive expressly for the carry line. This was No. 2, a saddle tank 0-4-0 switcher from the H. K. Porter Locomotive Works of Pittsburgh. Costing about five thousand dollars, it was similar to the small steam locomotives once used at industrial complexes and at mining and construction sites.

The singular difference between No. 2 and larger locomotives was that it had no tender. Instead, its coal supply bin was part of the cab itself. On such a short line it was easier to hand-fire the boiler from a supply of coal directly behind the engineer and fireman. A reserve supply was kept at coal pockets at each end of the line.

The railroad was never incorporated as a separate entity. At first it was a segment of Durant's Forest Park and Land Company development. Then it became a part of Durant's unincorporated Blue Mountain and Raquette Lake Steamboat Line.

A typical trip over the line might begin early on a summer morning when the overnight passengers from New York arrived at Raquette Lake in a Pullman car or day coach. Milling about the combination passenger and freight station, post office, and restaurant, they waited to board the narrow, double-decked steamboat, *Killoquah*, due to depart at 7 A.M.

The voyage across Raquette Lake and up the narrow and twisting Marion River consumed nearly an hour, the boat also stopped at some of the resorts and camps enroute. At the lower end of the Marion River Carry the train was always waiting when the steamer nosed her way upstream to pull alongside the dock. In short order

the boat was emptied and the train full. A few adventurous souls might cling to a stanchion, with one foot firmly planted on the running board.

The colorful red and white striped canvas awnings on the brown cars served a dual purpose. They could be let down in case of a sudden Adirondack storm. The front one, always in place, kept coal cinders from showering the passengers. If one did not wish to continue the trip to Blue Mountain Lake, excellent accommodations were offered at the Carry Inn, another of Durant's enterprises.

The engine puffed up past the train shed, flanges ringing on the gradual swing to the south along the side hill. There was usually a gasp when the train shot out onto the trestle. Then the cars swayed gently through another curve to the east, the river alongside now rapid and sparkling. Then came the dock at the Upper End and the trip was suddenly over before it had hardly begun.

There the steamer, *Tuscarora*, another double-decker, would be waiting to complete the boat run to the hotels on Blue Mountain Lake, and by a little past 9 A.M. William West Durant's goal of overnight service to and from New York City was now a reality.

Most visitors stayed a week or longer at one of the fashionable resorts. When the *Tuscarora* blew her departure whistle at 5:15 P.M., it was the last chance to make New York City by the next morning.

The spell of the Adirondacks led to quick friendships and close companionship. One man recalled:

"Sure, I met my wife on the carry. The train started up quick and she fell right in my lap. We got hitched in Utica the next day!"

Presidents of some of the great railroad systems of the United States traveled over the line at one time or another. These included E. H. Harriman of the Union Pacific, Collis

This 1911 postcard view shows the Marion River Carry Railroad mid-point between the upper and lower landings. (*Courtesy of Richard Palmer*)

P. Huntington of the Southern Pacific, and Patrick E. Crowley of the New York Central.

Other prominent summer visitors who rode the carry railroad included Henry Morgenthau Sr., ambassador to Turkey; Timothy L. Woodruff, lieutenant governor of the state of New York; and Anne Morgan, daughter of J. Pierpont Morgan.

George E. "Rassie" Scarritt was one of the early engineers (1902-1912) who coaxed No. 2 up and down the line. During the day the train crew of two or three were kept busy with shipments of freight and supplies for the camps and hotels which had been brought up to the carry by smaller line steamers and private launches.

Unique in the annals of Adirondack transportation were the car floats—long, flat, shallow-draft barges with rails spiked to the broad decks. A carload of coal, furniture, or merchandise could be delivered to the consignee's dock on Raquette Lake or billed through to the hotels on Blue Mountain Lake after being pushed up the carry from one float to another.

To a visitor to the Adirondacks it was startling to occasionally see the little steamer, *Irocosia*, chugging across Blue Mountain Lake, tugging a car float topped by a large Pennsylvania Railroad boxcar. One load of coal never reached its destination. The car float leaked, and well out into the lake it began to settle toward the rear. Startled deck hands heard a rumble and looked back, open-mouthed, as the float and car slowly rolled over and sank. It was never retrieved.

One of Durant's goals was to provide Pullman service through to Blue Mountain Lake. The boats and train could also bring the fabulous private cars of business magnates directly to the docks of their summer cottages and hunting lodges. Though the operation seemed entirely feasible, it

The car with no seats immediately behind the locomotive was used to haul canoes as well as baggage and mail. That's engineer C. P. Ives waving from the engine cab. (*Courtesy of Carl Haischer*)

was never implemented.

The Pullman Company and private car owners were, perhaps, skittish about having their cars winding up at the bottom of an Adirondack lake. Hence they never ventured beyond a siding at Raquette Lake village.

William Durant himself was described as having the dynamic qualities of a steam locomotive. But after bringing adequate transportation to the area, he was squeezed out. Due to a minor typhoid scare, the huge Prospect House at Blue Mountain Lake was closed. His golf course there did not make the money he expected, and Collis P. Huntington his financial mentor, died suddenly at his camp on Raquette Lake. Durant tried desperately to hold

Not much revenue freight or passengers the day this photo was taken of the Marion River Carry Railroad in the early 1900s. (*Courtesy of The Adirondack Museum*)

on, but broke and discouraged, he soon left the Adirondacks forever. Durant was forced to dispose of all his holdings in the region. The railroad and steamboat line went to a group headed by Dr. W. Seward Webb.

Ironically, another physician-turned-railroader pierced the mountains from the southwest. Dr. W. Seward Webb's St. Lawrence & Adirondack was pushed from Herkimer to Malone in 1891-92, penetrating the heart of the Adirondack region between Remsen and Tupper Lake.

Since he was the son-in-law of William H. Vanderbilt, Dr. Webb had the New York Central's financial backing in his bid to open the western Adirondacks. Soon, overnight service was established to the region from New York City via the New York Central. Sportsmen and summer vacationists flocked to the camps and many resorts established throughout the region after the railroad was completed.

Collis P. Huntington of the Southern Pacific also backed Webb who, in 1899, built the Raquette Lake Railroad. This stretched eighteen miles from Carter Station on the Mohawk & Malone to a terminus named "Durant" on the shores of Raquette Lake. But this was only the first step.

Under Webb, the steamboat line and its Marion River Carry Railroad were reorganized in the spring of 1901 as the Raquette Lake Transportation Company. Its board of directors consisted of some of the most prominent railroad and business magnates of the day including Henry P. Whitney, H. E. Huntington, John A. Dix, J. Pierpont Morgan, President Samuel Callaway of the New York Central, and Reginald Vanderbilt.

The moguls met annually in New York City to administer the routine affairs of the tiny Adirondack transportation line. Season after season the "millionaires' line" ran its combination route from Raquette Lake (formerly Durant) to Blue Mountain.

As the years passed more and more private camps were built on the lakes. Each summer between eight thousand and ten thousand passengers ascended and descended the twenty-seven-foot incline on the cars of the Marion River Carry Railroad. There were special one-day excursions out of Utica which taxed the capacities of both train and boats. On August 10, 1908, it is recorded that three hundred seventy-one people made the trip over the carry. The train made four shuttle trips each way that day.

In 1920, the whole Marion River Carry train was taken to Old Forge for winter storage where it was also refurbished. In 1923, the heirs of the original organizers of the Raquette Lake Transportation Company sold their interests to Maurice Callahan of Blue Mountain Lake, who had managed it for two decades. The operation also included a car float service between Raquette Lake and Forked Lake to accommodate the growing number of automobiles now penetrating the wilderness.

Callahan took no chances with loaded railroad coal cars and had loads transferred to a special light car that would not tax the older floats.

Winter froze the lifeline of the Marion River Carry, so its operations were confined to the months the steamboats operated. In spite of this limitation, the enterprise is said to have been a financial success from the very beginning. Across its right-of-way, carved through tall pines and bare tamaracks, the railroad's meager rolling stock for three decades handled between eight thousand and ten thousand passengers a year, in addition to freight traffic.

All told, the train could seat one hundred twenty-five passengers, but even then the "hoghead," or engineer, in later years Charles P. Ives or Chauncey S. Covey, sometimes had to make several trips to shuttle all the excursionists across the carry. On occasion, the railroad made special trips for people traveling through the lake region by canoe. The minimum tariff of one dollar for such trips probably stands as an all-time low record for the cost of chartering a special train.

Clyde Beals, in an article about the tiny railroad which appeared in the *New York Times* on August 19, 1928, wrote the following:

> The railroad line consists of a single stretch of track of a total length of seven-eighths of a mile. There are some switches at each end which might add a trifle to the trackage, but as a matter of local pride they are not counted. It serves only two stations, one at each end, though to reduce its activity to cold statistics is to depreciate its usefulness to its territory. It plays the part of the hole between two halves of an hourglass.
>
> Traffic gathers for it from large territories on each side and sometimes even strains its equipment, as many as 250 passengers often being carried in a day.

Weather-Beaten With Age

The engine looks much the same now as it did twenty-seven years ago when it took charge of the fleet, though a little more weather-beaten. The only visible change is one in the smokestack made by the present engineer, George Ripley, one-time fireman on the New York Central. He is a natural-born mechanic, according to his aide, Charles Walker. He does all the repairs necessary, the last trip to town for overhauling having been made five years ago. He decided shortly after taking over the run three years ago that the old stack was not well adapted to getting up steam in a hurry for a sudden call. He took two joints of kitchen stovepipe and fastened them on top by means of guy wires attached to strategic points on the boiler and elsewhere, giving it a stack still low enough to get under the trees, but high enough to insure a good draught.

Ripley puts the engine through several tricks that were not dreamed of in its birthplace. He drives down to the switch beside the Marion River and uses its steam in a pump to fill his water tower, which furnishes water for the engine and also for the dishwashing at his house in the station; and at other times he uses the steam to run a small buzz saw which keeps the house supplied with wood.

It was the automobile and improved roads that doomed the Raquette Lake Transportation Company. In 1929, the state highway from Raquette to Blue Mountain Lake, roughly paralleling the boat-train route, was built. The carry train made its last run on September 15, with James Proper at the throttle.

On September 19, Covey and another man were sent to the carry to lay-up the locomotive. On October 2, Covey, master mechanic for the Raquette Lake Transportation Company, sealed the locomotive and remaining car in the

This is a classic latter-day view of the little railroad as it neared the end of its life, taken by Liverpool photographer Ted Schuelke on August 28, 1927. It would run for only two more seasons.

enginehouse at the lower terminus. Years later, Covey ran the train at the Rail City Museum at Sandy Pond, near Pulaski, New York.

The Raquette Lake Transportation Company remained as a corporation for several years. The old engine and cars remained boarded-up in the long, high train shed. The rails went to a scrap dealer in 1939. Vandalism eventually stripped the silent shed where the train lay, half-forgotten.

It was known to hikers and canoeists only as "that old train in the woods."

A short walk over the roadbed of the old line today is a pleasant excursion into the past. Both docks are overgrown with brush, but bear traces of cinder ballast and soft coal. Notable is the big, unwieldy car float, half-submerged in Lake Utowana off the pier at the Upper End. About half the roadbed is still well-traveled by boating parties making the portage once more in the manner of the Indians and pioneers. The Carry Inn still exists, but as a private dwelling.

The railroad property was eventually acquired by Herbert A. Birrell of Raquette Lake, who donated what was left of the unique and famous train for a permanent exhibit at the Adirondack Museum. In the summer of 1955, the old 0-4-0 and car remains were loaded on a flatbed truck and hauled seven miles to the Adirondack Museum site on the hill above Blue Mountain. One passenger car was assembled from parts of the three, and the engine cosmetically restored by the museum staff. Wooden parts were reconstructed with the aid of old photographs.

The green, gold, red, black, and white paint job was done from the memories of men and women who had ridden the train in its heyday. The only item not restored was the missing builder's plate.

Since then, No. 2 and its Brooklyn horsecar have reposed beneath a train shed at the museum, where they have been seen by countless thousands of people. It is the most tangible evidence of the "shortest standard gauge railroad in the world."

Employees of the Marion River Carry Railroad were: John Hammond, George "Rassie" Scarritt, Jerut Little, John Slade, W. H. Horton, Harrison Linforth, Claude J. and Chauncey Covey, Elmer D. Jones, A. W. Harris, Floyd C. Brown, Charles P. Ives, George Ripley, Frank Tiernan, and James Proper.

LOCOMOTIVE ROSTER — MARION RIVER CARRY RAILROAD

No.	Builder	Bldr. No.	Type	Cyl. & Dr.	Disposition
1	Baldwin-7/1886	8049	0-4-0	14"x18"-48"	Unknown
	"Steam Dummy" Built 7/1886 for Suburban Rapid Transit Co. No. 4. Later Manhattan Railway #339. Sold to Forest Park & Land Co., 7/1899.				
2	Porter-8/1901	2396	0-4-0	11"x14"	Now at Adirondack Museum, Blue Mountain Lake, N.Y.

10

The Lowville & Beaver River Railroad

by Keith F. Maloney

The time was 1903. The place was the Lowville Club, built by Gilbert A. Blackmon, coal dealer, who was one of the village's leading citizens at that time.

While some of "the boys" were playing cards in the back room, or perhaps just talking, someone started discussing railroads. One thing led to another, and suddenly all those present had agreed that a railroad from Croghan to Lowville was just what was needed. Such an enterprise could haul the many dairy and forest products of the area.

Mr. Blackmon, himself, was present at the time. With all his usual energy and gusto he began to plan for the actual formation of a corporation that could get things started. Within a few weeks he had done just that.

A corporation was formed on August 3, 1903, for the purpose of building and operating a railroad from the county seat of Lewis County to Croghan. Through the late fall months and into the winter of 1903-04, Mr. Blackmon worked feverishly to corral stock subscriptions. His son, also named Gilbert, recalled the method his father used to secure these subscriptions. After collecting $11,000 from a few friends as a basis, he went by horse and buggy to the farm country north of the Black River. He'd walk into a farmer's home and say, "There a railroad coming through here and milk will be shipped to New York City; your total milk check will increase. Why, it'll haul all your produce and cattle out, and bring any goods you buy practically to your doorstep. The price is $100 per share. How much shall I put you down for?"

After a few hectic weeks of prodding and persuading the thrifty farmers of the region to part with their hard-earned money, the elder Blackmon had $60,000 in subscriptions.

Yet, because there still wasn't enough to cover preliminary expenses, Blackmon had to canvass Lowville and vicinity, where he obtained $50,000 from businessmen and townspeople. By then the stock totaled $110,000. Eventually the capital stock increased to $200,000.

On Thursday, February 4, 1904, an article appeared in Lowville's *Journal & Republican*. Attention was drawn to the rail venture and the writer painted a rosy prospect for the future. The greatest freight potential seemed to be dairy products, farm goods, and paper products from the J. P. Lewis mills in Beaver Falls, and tonnage from the numerous properties of Theodore Basselin, the biggest tim-

Gilbert A. Blackmon, founder of the Lowville and Beaver River Railroad.
(*Courtesy of Mrs. Gil Blackmon*)

the small settlement of New Bremen.

A controversy developed between the two rights-of-way; the company declaring the Watson route less desirable unless its residents subscribed more stock. In the next issue of the *Journal & Republican*, an unnamed resident of Watson stated that their route was best, and the length should be equalized, as the landowners of the proposed right-of-way were willing to give the land "free of charge." One might suspect some sort of a "deal" in this case, but in those days this was a basic tactic of railroad building.

By late spring surveyors were at work on the permanent line which was finally located in the town of New Bremen. Shortly afterward, the certificate of incorporation was published. During this period, both the New York Central and the Hudson River Railroad expressed "a friendly" interest in the welfare of the short line. A local company also offered to lease the road outright, using sev-

berland owner in the area except for Mr. Lewis. At the time, only a small number of subscribers were needed to complete the selling of stock. All stockholders were reported to be local people, mostly farmers and merchants.

By February 24, 1904, the initial capital stock had been subscribed, although the amount was later raised to cover construction costs. Practically everyone concerned with the project was enthusiastic, except for a few diehards who predicted outright disaster.

Spring arrived, and the surveying of rights-of-way was begun under the direction of C. E. Brownell of Carthage, New York. At first two routes were proposed. One—the final choice, ran from Lowville to the East Road, across the "flats" to the Illingsworth Bridge over the Black River, then to New Bremen. The alternate course went due east from the county seat to the mouth of Mill Creek, towards the hamlet of Watson and across the rolling countryside to

The office of Blackmon & Slack Company stood behind the area now occupied by the Lowville yard. (*Courtesy of Clarence Johnson*)

INCORPORATED UNDER THE LAWS OF THE
STATE OF NEW YORK

NUMBER 748

SHARES

THE LOWVILLE AND BEAVER RIVER RAILROAD COMPANY

LOWVILLE, NEW YORK

This Certifies that _____ is the owner of _____

Shares of the Capital Stock of

THE LOWVILLE AND BEAVER RIVER RAILROAD COMPANY

transferable only on the Books of the Corporation by the holder hereof in person or by duly authorized Attorney on surrender of this Certificate properly endorsed.

In Witness Whereof the duly authorized officers of this Corporation have hereunto subscribed their names and caused the corporate Seal to be hereto affixed at Lowville, N. Y.
this _____ day of _____ A. D. 19 _____

TREASURER

PRESIDENT

Shares $100. Each.

Old-time stock certificate. (*Courtesy of John Turnbull*)

Early L&BR switcher, aged and balky No. 51, acquired from the New York Central for use in construction. (*Courtesy of the Railroad Historical Society of Northern New York*)

eral bonds of large denomination. Both parties were treated with a polite "hands off" attitude.

At this time, the most noted and influential members of the board of directors were J. P. Lewis and Theodore Basselin. Prominent tradesmen of Lowville and well-to-do farmers of the area filled out the remainder of the group. Then, as throughout most of its history, much support in the form of carloadings and financial backing came from the J. P. Lewis Paper Company of Beaver Falls.

In the summer of 1904, James T. Campbell was awarded the contract for construction of the line, and the State Railroad Commission had approved all grade crossings. By late summer, a subcontract was let for the building of a trestle on the Black River flats. Italian laborers arrived shortly afterward and construction began. Soon after, they

all struck because their foreman had been fired. The railroad would have none of these shenanigans and sent them right back to New York City. A new work gang was speedily brought out and work resumed.

By November 17, 1904, work was progressing quite rapidly. The Lowville-New Bremen grading was almost completed and upwards of one hundred fifty men were on the job. Piles were also being driven for the Black River trestle. Later, fill was taken from the sandpit north of the Ebersol crossing in Beaver Falls and used to cover the trestle. As 1905 approached, piles were partially driven, and grading and track-laying were to begin in the spring.

During the winter, however, an unfortunate event occurred when James Campbell died. Frederick Easton and James Brownell took over the construction. According to

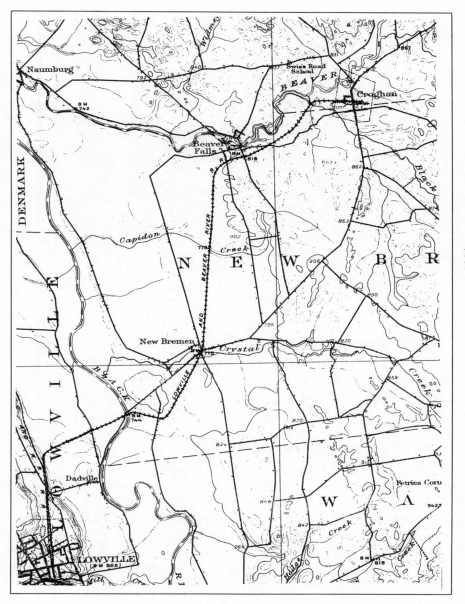

Map of the Lowville and Beaver River Railroad.

151

Splitting snowflakes on a mixed run in 1906 or '07 is No. 10. The long fill and steel trestle later replaced the wooden structure. (*Courtesy of Paul Schulz*)

old letters to board members, some difficulty was encountered in securing materials for bridge construction and in purchasing suitable locomotives. By the summer of 1905, however, everything was well in hand. Stations were being built, bridges erected, and track-laying was progressing satisfactorily.

In fact, though delays were encountered, strikes occurred and stock did not always sell like hotcakes, the L&BR had definitely arrived, come January 1906—with everything in readiness for the first run.

On January 13 one of Lowville's biggest days occurred. The *Journal & Republican* reported the event, with much enthusiasm, in its issue the following Thursday:

. . . . The Lowville and Beaver River Railroad is ten

and one-half miles in length. The heaviest grade on the road is two and one-half percent; the grade being almost entirely in the rise from the flatlands bordering the river to Lowville. The road is well-ballasted with sand and gravel, and sixty-pound (to the yard) rails are in use.

The approach to Black River from Lowville is over a 1,100-foot trestle constructed by Wisner & Sons, Lowville. The road crosses the river on a three-span iron and steel bridge built by the American Bridge Company. The weight of the bridge is two hundred tons and it cost $15,000. Heavy iron bridges also cross Crystal Creek at New Bremen and the Black Creek near Croghan.

The rolling stock of the road at present consists of four freight cars, two passenger coaches, and two engines, one a small shifting 0-4-0, No. 51, and the other a large passenger locomotive of a later type. (This was

152

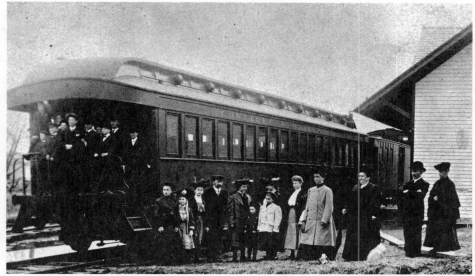

A group of passengers apparently ready to leave from Croghan. (*Courtesy of Mrs. Minnie Virkler*)

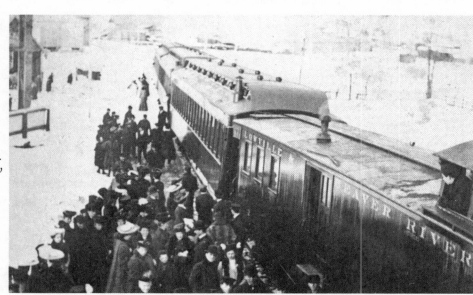

A large crowd at Lowville headed to Croghan. (*Courtesy of the Railroad Historical Society of Northern New York*)

The L&BR Railroad train bound for Lowville, standing at Beaver Falls depot in 1906. The engine, No. 3, was later numbered 10. The first engineer was "One-Eyed Dan" Clark. The conductor was Walt Goldthrite, probably the man on the steps of the caboose. The man with the buggy is probably Merritt Joyner, who ran the Beaver Falls Hotel and met the trains. Paper from the mills was loaded at the depot until the trestle and paper mill branch was completed in 1907. (*Courtesy of Ralph Van Arnam*)

from the Adirondack R.R., later part of the D.&H. System.)

The depot at Lowville, where the offices of the company are located, is a two-story brick building at one time used as a restaurant by the Rome, Watertown, and Ogdensburg railroad. The stations at New Bremen, Beaver Falls, and Croghan are constructed of wood, and, like the station at Lowville, are finished in the best of style. The stationmaster at Lowville has not yet been selected. Charles Bateman of New Bremen will be stationmaster at that place; Mr. French at Beaver Falls, and Jerard O'Brien at Croghan.

The train crew on the regular run at present consists of Walter Goldthrite, conductor; Daniel Clark ("One-eyed Dan"), engineer; and Philip Smith, fireman. The capital stock has been increased to $200,000. The total cost of the construction work, building stations, rolling stock, and all equipment is estimated at between $190,000 and $200,000.

At 9:00 A.M. Saturday the first excursion train, consisting of two coaches and a smoker, left Lowville. The roadbed was quite smooth and a crowd of three hundred enjoyed the trip thoroughly. At 1:00 in the afternoon, five hundred Croghanites arrived in Lowville, spent the afternoon, and returned home at 4:00 P.M.

The local paper congratulated the management on the way the crowd was handled, and credit was given to

Gilbert Blackmon, promoter and general manager, for his labors on behalf of the railroad. The writer forecast a prosperous future for the newly-born pike.

As with many short lines, the first ten years were the best for the little railroad. It was said that the vice president of the New York Central and Hudson River told one of the L&BR's directors that more milk and dairy products came from "his" railroad than at any point on the entire system. Business must have been very prosperous, indeed, at that time! Another Central official, the late railroad historian, Edward T. Hungerford, referred to the L&BR as a private line of the J. P. Lewis Company in his history of the RW&O. This statement, though incorrect at the time, certainly proved prophetic.

On Monday, January 15, 1906, the first paying passengers were carried and the official business of the L&BR began. The new business was off in a cloud of steamy smoke, a haze of cigar fumes, and was sent on its way with a round of hurrahs from local residents.

After the initial run, the Beaver River followed its first ceremonial excursion with a time card that featured several trains each way every day.

From the very first special commuter tickets were sold to students from outlying areas attending Lowville Academy. Here is a copy of the first timetable:

Exp.	Mixed	Mixed	Exp.			Exp.	Mixed	Mixed	Mixed
PM	PM	PM	AM			AM	AM	PM	PM
8:45	4:55	12:15	8:55	ar. CROGHAN	lv.	7:20	9:10	1:15	6:10
8:40	4:49	12:05	8:49	ar. B'FALLS	lv.	7:26	9:16	1:30	6:16
8:30	4:37	11:40	8:37	ar. N' BREMEN	lv.	7:38	9:30	1:50	6:28
8:15	4:20	11:20	8:20	lv. L'VILLE	ar.	7:55	9:50	2:15	6:45

9/9 G. A. BLACKMON, *Supt.*

That fall the first excursions to the fair began. They afforded an opportunity to visit Lewis County's Agricultural Exposition, whose biggest attraction was claimed to be its third annual horse show. The poster describing the fair didn't seem to be associated with the railroad, but after the first glance, it was easy to see that a list of rates and a schedule were included.

Lowville & Beaver River Railroad.
Time-Table No. 4, Effective 12:01 A. M., June 17th, 1906.

EAST.				DAILY EXCEPT SUNDAYS.		WEST.			
From Lowville Read Up.						To Lowville Read Down.			
EXP.	M'X'D	M'X'D	EXP.			EXP.	M'X'D	M'X'D	M'X'D
557	551	549	559			556	558	550	528
p. m.	p. m.	a. m.	a. m.			a. m.	a. m.	p. m.	p. m.
8.05	4.50	11.30	8.40	Ar.	CROGHAN.	Lv. 7.30	9.10	1.50	6.20
7.59	4.42	11.24	8.34	Lv.	BEAVER FALLS.	Lv. 7.36	9.16	1.56	6.26
7.52	4.35	11.17*	8.27	Lv.	NEW BREMEN.	Lv. 7.43	9.25	2.05	6.33
7.40	4.20	11.05	8.15	Lv.	LOWVILLE.	Ar. 7.55	9.50	2.25	6.45
p. m.	p. m.	a. m.	a. m.			a. m.	a. m.	p. m.	p. m.

Time subject to change without notice. G. A. BLACKMON, Gen'l. Supt.

When one passes through Croghan, it is sometimes noticed that a few of the businesses have 1912 cut or carved into their fronts. This is perhaps the only trace of one of the most sweeping disasters in North Country history, the fires that swept through Croghan in 1902 and 1905. They were followed by another in 1912, which was even more destructive. The latter holocaust might have engulfed the entire village, but according to local folklore, someone alerted the L&BR and the Lowville Fire Department.

By using the railroad, the Lowville firefighters arrived in time to help check the flames just short of the Franciscan Fathers' church and monastery. Sources claim the blaze had already reached its peak. In any case, the Beaver River was in some degree responsible for helping rescue a small town from being entirely wiped out.

Improvements to the railroad continued steadily. Al-

4 DAYS EXCURSION RATES 4
ON THE
Lowville & Beaver River Railroad
ON ACCOUNT OF THE GREAT
Lewis County Fair,

Forest Park, Lowville, N. Y.,
AUGUST 28th, 29th, 30th and 31st, 1906

LARGER AND BETTER THAN EVER!

$5,000 in Premiums and Purses! Special Exhibits of Thoroughbred Horses & Cattle

THIRD ANNUAL HORSE SHOW

30 Events, including several Novelties in the Horse Show line
never seen in Lewis County.

SPECIAL TRAIN SERVICE

On the Lowville and Beaver River Railroad, August 28th, 29th, 30th and 31st—Four Days Only.

Excursion tickets will be honored on following regular trains leaving Croghan 7:30 a. m. and 1:27 p. m., also on Special Train leaving Croghan 9:20 a. m; Beaver Falls, 9:25 a. m.; New Bremen, 9:35 a. m.

Returning, tickets will be honored on Regular Trains leaving Lowville 8:20 a. m., *4:20 p. m. and 7:40 p. m., and also on Special Train leaving Lowville 11:20 a. m.   Note *—This train will stop at Milk Station Crossing, near Fair Grounds, at 4:22 p. m., to pick up passengers.

SPECIAL LOW ROUND TRIP TICKETS will be on sale August 28th, 29th, 30th and 31st, only, as follows: Croghan, 50c.; Beaver Falls, 40c.; New Bremen, 25c.   Tickets will be honored on any regular train up to and including Saturday, September 1st.

G. A. BLACKMON, Gen'l. Supt.

Journal & Republican Print, Lowville.

though the volume of business warranted its being kept, the small "shifting" engine was scrapped, as it was continually derailing. This left one engine, the No. 10, an American-type 4-4-0 of high-stacked, loosely-coupled design, formerly of the Adirondack Railroad, where it was named the "C. F. Durkee" and carried the No. 3. This engine was built in 1870 at the Schenectady Locomotive Works.

As prosperity continued, one engine proved to be insufficient for the business at hand. So in 1912, two years before World War I, No. 1912, a bright new ten-wheeler 4-6-0 was built for the L&BR by the American Locomotive Company. It was the exact twin of an engine custom-built for the Glenfield and Western, a neighboring short line which hauled logs as a livelihood.

A new president, Jay S. Bowen, was elected in 1914. He took over from Theodore Basselin, who in turn had succeeded James P. Lewis. The L&BR's first president had been Charles P. Leonard.

In 1916, passenger business being heavier, the Beaver River contracted the then popular "doodlebug fever." This disease was prevalent from about 1910 until 1930. It afflicted many short lines, and was also caught by some of the larger rail systems. A "doodlebug" was a gasoline-engine-powered passenger coach. Many of them were cranky, fitful creatures; the "jitney" of the L&BR being no exception. It was purchased from the Salt Lake and Utah Railroad and was built by the Hall-Scott Company. Numbered 502, the jitney utilized a direct-drive gear transmission.

An individual acquainted with the railroad most of his life said this concerning its speed: "It may have ridden rough, but it sure could go like Hell!"

The "war to save democracy" brought a measure of

Aftermath of one of northern New York's greatest disasters—a $500,000 fire that leveled most of Croghan on April 30, 1912. (*Courtesy of Gerald Kirch*)

For a time, the station at New Bremen did a good business. It lost its agent in 1907 and remained open as a passenger shelter for several years. (*Courtesy of Mrs. Tina Farney*)

The station at Beaver Falls.
(*Courtesy of Mrs. Lena Hirschey*)

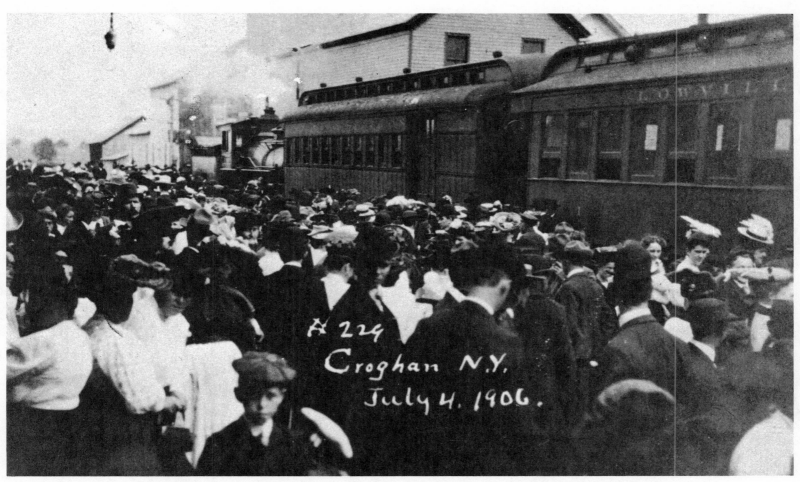

Folks gathered at the depot in Croghan on Independence Day, 1906. (*Courtesy of Leonard Virkler and S. H. Reeder*)

The No. 10, a classic American-type 4-4-0, chuffs away towards Croghan over a swing-type bridge built by the railroad to allow for steamboat and barge traffic on the Black River Canal. (*Courtesy of Leonard Virkler*)

The crew at Croghan. Left to right: Bennie Roth, pilot; Walt Goldthrite, conductor; Martin Just, baggageman; and "One-Eyed Dan" Clark, engineer. (*Courtesy of Mrs. Tina Farney*)

Lowville & Beaver River

RAILROAD

Time-Table No. 35
Effective 12:01 A. M., Dec. 1, 1917.

EAST-BOUND	Daily Except Sunday			Sunday Only	
LOWVILLE TO CROGHAN	29 Mxd. a. m.	5 Exp. p. m.	7 Exp. p. m.	33 Mxd. a. m.	9 Exp. p. m.
Lv. Lowville	9.40	4.15	7.30	9.37	6.55
Lv. New Bremen	9.58	4.30	7.45	9.53	7.10
Lv. Beaver Falls	10.10	4.39	7.54	10.03	7.19
Ar. Croghan	10.17	4.45	8.00	10.10	7.25

WEST-BOUND	Daily Except Sunday			Sunday Only	
CROGHAN TO LOWVILLE	2 Exp. a. m.	30 Mxd. p. m.	8 Exp. p. m.	10 Exp. a. m.	32 Mxd. p. m.
Lv. Croghan	7.50	1.40	5.50	8.00	12.45
Lv. Beaver Falls	7.56	1.47	5.55	8.05	12.51
Lv. New Bremen	8.05	1.58	6.04	8.14	1.01
Ar. Lowville	8.22	2.20	6.21	8.31	1.20

The time given herein is subject to change without notice.

G. A. BLACKMON, General Manager.

World War I-era timetable. (*Courtesy of Leonard Virkler*)

prosperity to Lewis County. Soldiers had been stationed at the various power developments on the Beaver River. This resulted in increased passenger revenue. Even in the days of the Liberty Bond drives and rallies, people of the area found enough time and money to take advantage of excursions offered during the year by the L&BR. The most popular were the trips to the Lewis County Fair in the fall. The excursions featured flatcars equipped with benches and trimmed with cedar boughs, in addition to regular passenger coaches and "jitney."

Once the war was over, and after a brief recession, one of the biggest booms in our nation's history began to gain momentum. It affected the L&BR in a big way. First, the old No. 10 locomotive was retired in 1920 after many years' service on the rails of the north country. Then, in 1923, the Beaver River bought an oil-burning steam engine from the Paterson, New Jersey shops of the American Locomotive Company. Originally destined for a South American "banana republic," this long-boilered Consolidation 2-8-0 was converted to coal, and actively served the L&BR until 1947. It was stored at Lowville until 1964.

In 1925, due to the upward spiral of revenues, dividends were paid on common stock. This happy event continued, with the exception of one year, until the late 1950s. According to a magazine article, the L&BR was the only railroad in the United States to pay a dividend during the depression years. If true, it was an enviable record.

At this same time construction was begun on the Soft Maple, High Falls, and Moshier Falls power developments. The huge number of men, equipment, and material needed to build these large dams was hauled, in large part, by way of the Lowville road.

The late Paul Schulz, a farmer and railroad enthusiast from New Bremen, recalled seeing penstock sections be-

In this classic view No. 10 is headed south to Lowville, just before tackling the two and a half percent grade up Limekiln Hill. Postmark on the original postcard is October 22, 1907, when the line was less than two years old. (*Courtesy of Mrs. Tina Farney*)

Old "jitney" gas car of L&BR is duplicated in this HO-gauge model, built by Model Engineering Works, Monrovia, California. Lowville road's "jitney" was bought from the Salt Lake & Utah. (*Courtesy of Model Railroad & Hobby Center, Syracuse*)

ing doubleheaded through that village by the two L&BR engines, Nos. 1923 and 1912. According to Paul, these construction trains sometimes had as many as twenty or twenty-five cars. To others acquainted with the line, this sounds like a rather staggering number.

Long-time residents claim there was seldom a dull moment on the little pike during the 1920s, especially if you count all the incidents, anecdotes, and outright "whoppers" about the jitney. According to the *Watertown Standard* of February 12, 1925, this is what happened to the jitney one dark, foggy night:

Fifty Persons Are Saved by Walter O'Brien

Stopped Train From Passing Over Dangerous Railroad Trestle Due to High Water . . . Man ran mile and a half to Beaver Falls to spread alarm—Supports of trestle weakened by high water.

(Special to the *Standard*)

Lowville, Feb. 12 — Fifty persons, about 25 of whom were students, riding on the train of the Lowville-Beaver River Line between this place and Croghan, owe their lives to Walter O'Brien, an employee of the Black River Power Corporation, who averted what might have been one of the most disastrous accidents in the (history of) the North Country railroads Wednesday afternoon.

O'Brien discovered a washout at the trestle, a mile this side of Croghan, and notified the railroad authorities in time to stop the train before it crossed the trestle. One of the main supports of the trestle had settled about a foot in the soft embankment that had been partly washed away by the high floodwaters of the Black Creek.

O'Brien was on his way from High Falls to Beaver Falls, and was walking on the tracks when he reached the trestle (Croghan side) and saw the dangerous condition that resulted from the high floodwaters. The bridge part of the trestle is about fifty feet long. The last train had been through about one in the afternoon and at that time the trestle was in good condition. O'Brien realized that another train (the jitney) was due in a few minutes and he ran a mile and a half into Beaver Falls, reaching there just as the train was about to proceed in the direction of the trestle. O'Brien was exhausted from the run, but earned the warm praise and appreciation of railroad

Lewis Co. Fair Lowville, N.Y.

Mandeville, Photo.

Special runs to the Lewis County Fair were a well-known service of the L&BR. Mandeville was a prolific regional photographer of the time. (*Courtesy of Richard Palmer*)

officials and the passengers.

The Lowville & Beaver River Line is only a short one but a valuable one to the persons living in the small towns in this region. Students of the local (Lowville) high school use the line with advantage to get back and forth from their homes and the train was crowded with them yesterday afternoon. The train, in addition to stopping at Beaver Falls, also stops at New Bremen and Croghan. The students will not be able to get to school here until the trestle is strengthened. State and country (sic) roads do not lead to most of their homes and country roads are nearly impassable . . .

The news article then told of the jitney and its crew, Roy Williams and Eugene Edwards. It also claimed, incorrectly, that heavy rainfall and melting snow alone were responsible for damage to the Black Creek bridge.

Actually, the fill adjoining the Croghan side of the structure was washed-out because of a woodchuck hole, presumably dug the previous fall. Snow from the Croghan yards had been dumped so that it ran out through the burrow during thaws, causing the washout, not high water and floating ice floes, as the *Standard* claimed. As an appropriate aftermath Mr. O'Brien was later awarded a total of $390 by grateful citizens and the train crew.

The L&BR had several mishaps including grade crossing accidents and employee injuries.

Another time the jitney—again carrying students and shoppers—was derailed during the 1920s on Limekiln Hill near Lowville. The Croghan-bound freight train, pulled by No. 1923, had spread the light rails at the base of the grade. As the freight was slow in returning to Lowville, the jitney was sent after it to see what was going on. When the jitney rounded the turn it "went aground," and once out on the fill crossing the Black River flats, tipped over.

All was confusion inside. A coal stove, luckily bolted securely to the floor, stayed put and saved lives of all on board by doing so. The jitney, like many older coaches, wasn't exactly fireproof. All passengers escaped by following the lead of a New Bremen youth named Martin who, forgetting that the floor was now the windows, fell through one of them, cutting himself extensively.

Theodore Rohr was the conductor on the run. He knocked out the rest of the window Martin had fallen through, checked to make sure it was relatively safe passage, then herded the remaining passengers out this improvised escape hatch. They joined the crew and others who had broken out their own windows, dropping to the ground beneath the keeled-over jitney. The group then walked back to Lowville in the chilly winter weather.

The late 1920s were good years for the Beaver River, but with the Great Depression came hard times, more motor trucks on the roads, and a general reduction in revenues. One bright spot lit these years, however. On April 1, 1930, $35,000 in preferred stock was retired and paid off. This dated back to pre-construction days and eliminated the problem of funded debt.

Unfortunately, from then on the fortunes of the line took a negative turn. On September 7, 1933, Gil Blackmon, the promoter and general manager since 1906, passed away. A New York Central official, Thomas Dorsey, arrived shortly after to manage the affairs of the railroad. By this time the nation was in the depths of the greatest "bust" it had ever faced, with railroads especially hard hit. Many succumbed to the clutches of bankruptcy and receivership, but not the L&BR. Despite the increasing age of its motive power, property depreciation, and income losses, the L&BR came through this bleak period financially and physically whole.

Windsor and Kellogg House cabs and fancy carriage await northbound Central express just pulling in. L&BR main station in the background was once the RW&O eating house. (*Courtesy of Leonard Virkler*)

Engine No. 1912 attempting to make its own roadbed just north of Beaver Falls on February 20, 1917. (*Courtesy of Minnie Virkler*)

This photo is "doctored." The portion on the right is indeed Croghan station, but note the hairline split next to the water plug. The changes became apparent when the original postcard was enlarged. The smoking locomotive was evidently photographed on the New York Central line, years after the Croghan picture was taken. (*Courtesy of Paul Schulz*)

Another altered postcard featuring agent Martin Just and Beaver Falls depot. Such products were created by the Beach photo studio in Remsen, noted for amusingly "improved" pictures of north country communities, railroads, and resorts. (*Courtesy of Sidney Herzig*)

In 1938, Jay S. Bowen was replaced as president by Fay L. Parker, whose administration accomplished several important things. First, even though the World War II period was a lean one for the Beaver River, locomotives were kept running, track was relaid with heavier rail, and generally the property began to look better.

It was about this time that railfan Charles Vineall visited the Lowville railroad, and was so pleased with what he found that he wrote a few lines to *Railroad Magazine*. The results appeared in the November 1942 issue. Vineall asked readers,

Who can tell me whether or not the L&BR, 10½ mile standard gage line in New York State, is the only one

which numbers locomotives by the dates they were built? I learned the facts on a recent visit to this road. There are two L&BR engines, built by Alco: No. 1912, a 4-6-0 type built that year, now stored at Lowville, N.Y., and No. 1923, a Consolidation, built that year, now in daily service, but still bearing heat marks on her tender-plate from a fire which nearly destroyed her years ago.

The fire referred to by Vineall had taken place about 1938, according to the recollections of retired L&BR chief engineer, Earl Rennie. Rennie, who started his career running a steam-powered highway roller for the Lewis County Highway Department, later became a fireman for the now defunct Glenfield & Western. Upon the demise of that logging line, he moved to the Lowville operation. He remembered that the fire took place in the middle of a bitter cold north country winter, and almost melted the

Lewis Paper Mill, Beaver Falls. (*Courtesy of Sidney Herzig*)

Residences shown here were originally built by the Lewis firm for employees years ago. It is known locally as "Toytown." (*Courtesy of Sidney Herzig*)

The former Lewis mansion at Beaver Falls. (*Courtesy of Sidney Herzig*)

The county court house dominates a stretch of State Street in the village of Lowville where the Beaver River line connects with the MA&N. (*Courtesy of Richard Palmer*)

No. 1923 in its roundhouse. Fortunately, however, the 2-8-0 was reclaimed from the flames, though much welding, sheet metal work, and brasswork was needed to restore it to running condition.

Returning to Vineall's letter, he stated:

The L&BR is one of the few roads left in this state which has a steady income. It runs between Lowville, (the) New York Central connecting point, and Croghan.

Besides giving farmers access to metropolitan markets, it serves paper mills and a block factory (Croghan.)

Rolling stock includes several flatcars, a wedge snowplow, and a combination baggage and express coach (the jitney); formerly used on a Western electric interurban line. The company has four depots, all pleasing in appearance; also its headquarters, a water tank (since moved to a rail museum), a two-stall enginehouse and a hand-operated turntable.

NOTICE

THE LOWVILLE AND BEAVER RIVER RAILROAD
COMPANY HEREBY GIVES NOTICE THAT ON
AND AFTER DECEMBER 1st, 1946, IT WILL
DISCONTINUE ALL PASSENGER SERVICE
ON ITS LINE.

THE PUBLIC SERVICE COMMISSION OF THE
STATE OF NEW YORK WAS ADVISED OF
THIS ACTION ON OCTOBER 29, 1946.

By Order of the Board of Directors.

The handwriting on the wall, the L&BR abandons passenger service just after the end of World War II. (*Courtesy of Leonard Virkler*)

Shortly after the war, as L&BR President Fay Parker later recalled, "Passenger service was continued until January 10, 1947; there was seldom a passenger to serve because of the increasing number of automobiles and trucks, and the added expense of maintenance and hauling coach for no revenue was unwarranted."

Notice of this sad event was taken in the *Lowville Leader* of January 10, 1947. Editor John Boyd noted some interesting facts about the little line—the most surprising being that it once carried 144 passengers in one day!

In May of 1947, a 44-ton, center-cab, diesel-electric locomotive arrived from the Erie, Pennsylvania shops of General Electric. An attractive unit with a striking maroon and yellow color scheme, it was sometimes slightly underpowered for the steep grade of 2.5 percent on Limekiln Hill.

The 4-6-0, No. 1912, was sold when the GE took over, and for several years the other Alco 2-8-0 sat in the roundhouse. Be that as it may, the diesel helped keep the road competitive. In fact, the small short line improved its physical plant, track, etc. so that it was solvent and modestly prosperous until late in the 1950s.

A chime airhorn was installed on the No. 1947 about 1952, following the first fatal grade-crossing accident on the road in thirty years. The mishap caused the death of M. J. Kessler of Castorland, New York, and happened at the Illingsworth Bridge crossing. Despite the unfortunate reason for its installation, the No. 1947's whistle was appreciated by railfans, for its melodic tones were similar to a steamer's whistle.

For four months in mid-1954, old engine No. 1923 was hauled out of the roundhouse for general freight service on a regular daily basis—replacing the diesel when its electrical system was due for overhauling.

Engine No. 1923 in Lowville yard, next to the water tank. (*Courtesy of the Railroad Historical Society of Northern New York*)

Typical winter scene in the 1950s and early '60s, before shrinking traffic and revenues eliminated the carrying of small shipments in the traditional red caboose. (*Courtesy of Paul Schulz*)

It is pleasant to recall No. 1923 as it stood, with air pumps hissing and clunking, and with steam issuing from various odd places, in front of the depots in Croghan or Beaver Falls on those hot July and August days. A typical consist of the L&BR back then would have been: the venerable Alco and its tender (still sporting marks from that near-disastrous fire in the 1930s); a boxcar which had carried feed to Farney's mill or the Croghan G.L.F.; or a GATX tank car filled with liquid rubber for Latex Fiber Industries, Inc., a Beaver Falls industry, principal sources of revenue for the L&BR.

At the rear of this modest string of cars would come a piece of rolling stock which was stored, still serviceable, at the Lowville roundhouse—a former Lehigh Valley Railroad caboose, painted the inimitable barn red, having a bit of yellow trim and featuring arch-bar trucks. A notable detail of this "crummy" (not lost on railfans) was its distinctive side door, something long departed from most main and short line units. The caboose dutifully brought up the rear of all freights until the loss of Express/LCL

(less-than-carload) shipments. It was sold a few years later.

That summer many of the old-time employees were still working on the railroad, including the late Martin F. Just, station agent and coal dealer at Beaver Falls since about 1906; Arthur Artz, foreman of the track gang; and a Mr. Jackson, a former fireman turned trackman.

Steam's last stand on the Lowville line came in the cold and savage winter of 1957. On a sub-zero January morning, it was found that the diesel would not respond. So with, one supposes, appropriately warm comments to suit the extremely cold weather, the veteran railroaders of the L&BR managed to fire up the rusty boiler of the 2-8-0.

With a variety of squeaks, moans, chuffs, and rattles, the old steamer, with billowing clouds of vapor issuing from practically every pore, made the trip to Croghan and the return for several days. Because of the boiler's temperamental and cranky behavior, the crew doubtlessly was grateful when the warm cab of the GE 44-tonner (with its wrap-around view and windshield wipers) was restored to them.

174

Despite the departure of the old steam locomotive, the Lowville line still looked much as it had in the past. Its small yards, weathered but serviceable buildings, and loyal employees were representative of small-time American short line railroading.

This provincial rail link with the past has served northern Lewis County well for six and a half decades.

During the mid-1950s these were the officers of the Lowville & Beaver River: Fay L. Parker, president; Julius Farney, Croghan, vice president; Joseph M. Russum, treasurer; and Milton E. Burhans, secretary and operating superintendent. Mr. Burhans had been with the railroad since the early 1940s.

Other board members, reflecting ownership of stock in the line among farm families of the region and industrialists, were: James P. Lewis (grandson of the J. P. Lewis who was on the original board in 1904) and Dewitt C. LeFevre, Beaver Falls; Norbert V. Steiner, Castorland; Nathaniel E. Merrell, G. Byron Bowen, John D. Dence, H. Northam Haberer, and Varner M. Lyman, Lowville; and Norman J. Farney, Croghan.

A principle source of revenue for the L&BR was J. P. Lewis and Latex and Fiber Industries in Beaver Falls. Also, Farney's feed mill in Croghan and the A.M.F. block mill in Croghan contributed some carloadings. In the mid-1950s Beaverite Products, Inc., Beaver Falls, had some LCL and express business, but this was not substantial.

With declining income the railroad's directors, then headed by G. Bryon Bowen, president, realized they represented a widely-scattered group of shareholders. They were "faced with the problem of liquidating the railroad or finding a buyer," and after careful deliberation it was decided that ownership by the Lewis interests would be appropriate and negotiations were begun.

In 1943 railfan G. L. Barrett found old 4-6-0 No. 1912 waiting out its remaining years in the Lowville enginehouse. (*Courtesy of Leonard Virkler*)

Making one of its last appearances, No. 1923 was welcomed by children as it steamed through New Bremen. (*Courtesy of Vernon Windover*)

Steam's last stand on the Lowville pike came in 1957. No. 1923 is shown pushing through light snow towards Lowville, as it crossed the Black River flats. (*Courtesy of Alice Virkler*)

Tom Root of Plymouth, Ohio, captured No. 1923 on film shortly before its departure for the Steamtown Rail Museum. At left is a portion of an old snowplow used by the L&BR, built by the Russell Snow Plow Company, Brockway, Pennsylvania, and formerly of the Skaneateles Railroad. (*Courtesy of Leonard Virkler*)

Minus its cowcatcher, No. 1923 leaves Lowville in mid-1964 bound for the Steamtown, USA museum in New England. (*Courtesy of the Watertown Daily Times*)

At the time of the takeover there were 1,405 shares outstanding, on which a $2.00 dividend had been paid each year until 1959.

As a result of negotiations, the Beaver River Power Corporation, (a Lewis subsidiary named for its hydro plants on the river of the same name), bought almost every share of stock for $80.00 per. Beaver River Power actually held 1,385 shares and J. P. Lewis Company retained the eighty-six it had already. Seventeen shares were still outstanding, tied up in estates, etc.

Following several reorganizations, as of 1959, corporate officers of the road were: Dr. E. A. Harvey, executive vice president of the J. P. Lewis Company, president; Sam R. Phillips, general manager of the Latex Fiber Industries mill, vice president; A. John Turnbull, treasurer of J. P. L., treasurer; Richard Cummings, J. P. L.'s secretary and general manager, secretary; and Leonard K. Virkler, assistant treasurer. Directors were James P. Lewis, Mary L. Groat (Lewis' sister, who served as president of the line for a time during the 1960s), and Cummings.

New equipment included another 44-ton diesel from the Louisville & Nashville in 1963, two new rail maintenance cars from the Reading, and a brand new office next to the diesel house (replacing the hard-to-heat offices in the ancient but historic RW&O eating house, across the tracks from the former NYC station). Track reconditioning, tie replacement, weed control, and repainting programs were also implemented.

The Lewis Company counsel, Attorney Richard Cummings, related that in 1958 or 1959 the New York Central had given up the milk-carrying business in the north: "Of course, delivery of milk was one of our primary factors in traffic."

In 1963, after realizing the line was a losing proposition for Beaver River Power, the new owners petitioned the New York State Public Service Commission to sell its interests to J. P. Lewis and Latex Fiber, the concerns making up most of its business of wood pulp bales, waste paper, resin, chemicals in bulk, coal, rags, and liquid latex.

In mid-1965, another change in ownership took place. The Lewis Company and Latex split ownership of the rail subsidiary more or less fifty/fifty so that gains or losses shown would be equally felt by the two firms.

The new owners of the Beaver River Line made many significant improvements. Superintendent and general manager Leonard K. Virkler, a former independent businessman and past mayor of Lowville, helped increase efficiency by reducing the number of employees from about twenty-five to approximately six people.

The road's regular employees, in mid-1972, were: William Brown, engineer; Bernard Martin, conductor; David Norton, brakeman and apprentice engineer; Allan Pominville, track foreman; and John Czimar, trackman.

However, by 1976, carloadings had dropped to an average of two per day. The line then handled a total of 24,530 tons of freight—grain, coal, pulp, latex, waste pa-

After its arrival at Steamtown, No. 1923 was "prettied up" by the museum's management, but was not operable. (*Courtesy of Al Kallfelz*)

per for recycling, asbestos, and rags.

But by far the biggest news in the early and mid-1970s concerning the little railroad came from the fact that it had more ownership changes. As previously noted, the J. P. Lewis and Latex firms each owned roughly half the stock of the line in 1973. That year, A. John Turnbull, an executive with the Lewis Company, became president, with Sam R. Phillips, who headed the Latex operations in Beaver Falls, as vice president. Richard Cummings was secretary and J. J. Eagan, controller of Latex, was now treasurer. The changes reflected Latex Fiber's takeover of J.P. Lewis in 1973, and its acquisition of outstanding L&BR stock.

Lowville and Beaver River diesel No. 1947 at J. P. Lewis Mill, Beaver Falls.

Illingsworth Bridge crossing.

Climbing Limekiln Hill near Lowville.

Crossing the bridge over the Black River. (*Photos by Richard Palmer*)

Number 1950, purchased from Louisville & Nashville in 1963, as it crossed the trestle on Mill Branch over the Beaver River. (*Courtesy of Leonard Virkler*)

Leaving Croghan yards with a single flatcar. (*Photo by Richard Palmer*)

A last look at the L&BR as the abbreviated train trundles towards Croghan. (*Photo by Richard Palmer*)

Then, in an even more significant corporate development that affected the northern Lewis County economic picture and business climate, as well as the short line, the Boise Cascade Corporation, a giant forest products concern headquartered in Boise, Idaho, acquired Latex Fiber Industries in 1977, as well as Latex control and ownership of the L&BR.

Application to the Interstate Commerce Commission to gain control of the little railroad was made by Boise Cascade in mid-April 1977. In Finance Docket No. 28415, the ICC approved the move, noting among other things that the new owners also operated the Valley & Siletz Railroad Company, "an Idaho intrastate rail carrier," and the "Minnesota, Dakota & Western Valley Railway, which was a Minnesota intrastate rail carrier." The ICC docket also stated that there were "two shippers and/or receivers of freight located along the right-of-way, and no other rail service in competition."

The purchase price of the one, it was noted, was $55,441, covering ninety-nine percent of the capital stock (eighteen shares of which could still not be located). The ICC found Boise Cascade "fit, financially and otherwise, to consummate the transaction as proposed."

In an initial report, the new members of the L&BR referred to it as a "transportation subsidiary of Boise Cascade." The Lowville and Beaver River had survived in name, and somewhat in corporate structure, despite all the business and financial reshuffling of the past two decades.

As of December 1977, Leonard Virkler had retired as general manager and assistant treasurer; Dale Brown had replaced Bernard Martin as conductor; and Lawrence Leviker became track foreman, succeeding Allen Pominville. Neil and Stephen Birchenough were listed as section hands, instead of John Czimar, now a trackman.

According to information provided by Mr. Turnbull, now general manager of the L&BR, in addition to his main position as manager of transportation and shipping for Boise Cascade's Latex fiber products division, officers of the line were R. H. Schwarz, president, and R. W. Walters, vice president. There were three other vice presidents as well, plus five other corporate officers, most of whom were not only Boise Cascade's management people, but simultaneously served as officers of the company's other transportation and rail interests or subsidiaries. As of early 1978, a board of directors had yet to be named for the L&BR, but its days of being financially, if not operationally, controlled by primarily locally-based industrial concerns and individuals had ended.

Fresh coats of Boise Cascade green and white paint covered many of the original barn-red L&BR buildings in the beginning of 1978. The office was relocated from Lowville to Beaver Falls and Boise Cascade's "Lewis" mill. Otherwise, seemingly little had changed, at least on the surface.

Behind the scenes, however, overhead costs of running even this small railroad were continually rising, property taxes being the heaviest burden.

In October 1985, *Railpace Newsmagazine* carried a cover feature on the Lowville line written by Jack Wright. Wright cited the L&BR as "one of the most obscure short lines in upstate New York." He observed that the L&BR's "future depends upon the vitality of the Boise Cascade mill. At present, that future looks secure, but the past has taught us never to be cocksure. As long as Boise Cascade remains active, the little L&BR will continue to roll."

Four more years passed under Boise Cascade's ownership and still the line's basic routine remained as it had for decades. Dick Bonci was transportation manager at Boise Cascade, overseeing the line's operations. David Norton of Lowville was engineer and, aided by other Boise Cascade employees, took care of maintenance on the two GE 44-tonners. Unfortunately, time and corporate trends were about to catch up with the little pike.

Setting a series of negative events in motion was the sale by Boise Cascade of its Lewis County properties to a new firm, Specialty Paperboard. This company was owned by former Boise Cascade executives, with Boise Cascade retaining a minority interest in it. The new regime, though not actively opposed to continuing rail service, soon discovered that overhead costs were becoming too great. They considered themselves to be papermakers, not railroaders, a logical enough position.

Meanwhile Livingston Lansing, a Boonville businessman and railroad enthusiast, purchased the Shay No. 8 from an Arkansas railroad. It arrived at Rome Locomotive Works, on April 18, 1989, with much fanfare. Even the trucker who hauled the ancient steamer reported that he and his cargo were the subject of countless home videos and snapshots taken by passersby all along the route north.

At various times during the summer of 1989, Ed Schnabl, Peter Gores, former trainmaster on the Rochester & Southern, and this writer all met with Liv Lansing, and they suggested the L&BR as a possible site for the Shay.

Schnabl, during his research, had discovered that there were only 3,100 Shays built since the first prototype was constructed in Michigan by designer Ephraim Shay in 1877. What had been needed was a locomotive that could provide hours of continuous service, had the ability to climb steep grades, had sufficient pull and traction to deliver long loads of raw timber, and that would be surefooted on poorly-laid tracks. The unique, gear-driven design of the Shay was perfect for the job.

By the fall of 1989, the Lansing group discovered that locomotive rebuilding was becoming increasingly complex and an extremely costly proposition. Initial estimates put the cost of rehabilitating the Shay at $150,000, however, sources familiar with the process believed that it would end up being far costlier.

At about the same time, Specialty Paper had decided that it was costing too much to keep the L&BR running, reportedly putting them in the red to the tune of over $200,000 annually.

On November 1, 1989 the *Lowville Journal & Republican* dropped a bombshell onto the Lewis County rail scene, "Rail freight service to Lewis County may soon be a thing of the past if Conrail has its way. Conrail has recently published a list of thirteen lines that are candidates for abandonment over the next three years. Included in the list is the Lowville Industrial Track, milepost 58.1 to 74.1, from Carthage to Lowville."

Rome Locomotive Works had decided by that time, as well, that they wanted to expand into the rail operations business. For a time they showed an interest in not only obtaining the L&BR, but also in obtaining the connecting Conrail industrial track from Lowville to Carthage.

Events began to move quickly. In December 4, 1989, a public meeting was convened by the county Chamber of Commerce and held in Lowville. Potential buyers, local shippers, rail employees, and a representative of the New York State Department of Transportation attended.

At this critical point, Peter Gores had been working with friends and associates in the Genesee Valley Transportation Co. David J. Monte Verde, president; and vice presidents Jeffrey P. Baxter, Charles Reidmiller, Michael Thomas, and John Herbrand, in an effort to purchase the L&BR. They welcomed the Lansing group as an integral part of any L&BR/Lowville Industrial Track purchase.

Close-up of L&BR Railroad's "Armstrong" turntable, with No. 1950 and former RF&P No. 804 coach in the background. (*Courtesy of Maurice F. Switzer*)

Whether by coincidence or design, Specialty Paper added to the latter-day drama of the L&BR by arranging for its abrupt operational demise just as the planning for its purchase and restoration was gaining momentum.

The last run of the L&BR under Specialty was in January 1990. Neil Birchenough was the engineer and Joe Anderson, the conductor. Other employees at the time included David Norton, his son David Jr., and Larry Leviker.

For the first time since January 13, 1906, the L&BR rail line ceased regular revenue operation. Rust now began to coat the rails between Lowville, Beaver Falls, and Croghan. Weeds rose unchecked in the Lowville yards.

Just a few weeks before that, Larry Malski, a rail attorney and consultant, had been retained by Liv Lansing and the Genesee Valley Transportation (GVT) group to put together a creative proposal to insure a lower cost of owning and operating the L&BR for its next proprietor.

At the same time, Lewis County Industrial Development Authority became a part of the chain of negotiations which was moving toward a new era for the short line.

Ironically, even as the line was shut down, Malski was orchestrating a plan that proved critical to the project.

His proposal called for a ten percent ownership interest by Liv Lansing in the L&BR, in conjunction with ninety

Shay No. 8 in the Lowville yard, spotted on the new connecting track between L&BR's original terminal tracks and the former NYC-Conrail sidings. (*Photo by Keith F. Maloney*)

percent by Genesee Valley Transportation. A meeting introducing this concept to Specialty Paper took place on January 12, 1990. The proposal "opened the door," according the Ed Schnabl, who looked back on it as "the turning point." Present were: Bruce Moore, Specialty Paper president, Malski, Liv Lansing, David Monte Verde, Jeff Baxter, Pete Gores of GVT, Ed Schnabl, and Olivia Shoemaker.

This purchase offer on the L&BR coincided with Genesee Valley Transportation's deal with Conrail involving the sale of the Lowville-Carthage branch (LIT).

This very important move allowed GVT to rescue rail service to and from Lowville from the ash heap. It is reported by GVT personnel that Conrail executives acknowledged that the GVT/Acquisition Group's purchase of the L&BR prevented the outright abandonment of the Lowville to Carthage connecting branch by Conrail.

External appearances can be misleading. A visitor to Lewis County in February 1990 would have seen just another apparently abandoned railroad bed with snow covering its rusty rails. Trucks were now being used to supply the mills along the Beaver River.

In a communique sent in early July 1990, David J. Monte Verde, GVT president, informed the County Industrial Development Authority:

> In our July 2nd letter to Mr. Bruce Moore, we put forth the actions necessary to move the ownership of the L&BR from Specialty Paper Industries to Lewis County's ownership for tax relief. Following the transfer, the Group requires the empowerment to act as the County's sole Agent for the lease and operation of the Railroad.

185

L&BR and MA&N locomotives and rolling stock fill the Lowville yard. (*Courtesy of Maurice F. Switzer*)

Thus, as Pete Gores and Livingston Lansing had been searching for a location for a steam tourist operation in the north country, the principals of the Depew, Lancaster & Western Railroad had been working through Conrail on possible acquisition of the Lowville Industrial track, with the idea of also purchasing the L&BR. When both parties realized they were pursuing similar goals, they formed the Lowville and Beaver River Railroad Acquisition Group.

For the next several months, Lansing's group became enmeshed in Shay boiler repair/rebuild problems. Finally, in September 1990, the old Lima-built boiler was sent to Dillon Boiler Works in Fitchburg, Massachusetts, where it was labored over for nine months before being returned to the Rome shops. Here the boiler was reattached to the

Shay. Tests were run, with people from the boiler factory at Fitchburg in attendance. Leakage problems were encountered, and the Lansing group was not very satisfied with the way things were working out.

On September 18, 1990, Peter Gores, now involved with GVT as its prospective Lowville resident general manager, called Lansing's office and announced that the L&BR "deal" was close to completion.

By October, GVT formed the Mohawk and Adirondack Railroad. (This was later changed to the Mohawk, Adirondack and Northern.) GVT thus purchased and operated former Conrail lines from Carthage to Lowville, Carthage to Newton Falls, and Lyons Falls to Utica, a total of 117 miles.

Liv Lansing was asked to fund part of the expanded venture. In turn he received ten percent ownership in the MA&N as well as the L&BR. By late fall, Olivia Shoemaker was Lansing's representative for the negotiations.

The following information was obtained, in 1991, through meetings with Specialty Paper Industries' Bruce Moore and his personnel:

> The data pointed to the fact that if rail service on the L&BR was to be restarted, certain economic and operational changes would have to be enacted.
>
> 1) The Acquisition and financing of the line would have to be reasonable, for the railroad could not support a heavy debt service.
>
> 2) The number of personnel employed the railroad would have to be reduced considerably.
>
> 3) If the Group acquired the railroad, it will be necessary for a principal of the Group to relocate to Lewis County and become a resident manager of the operation.
>
> 4) All property taxes would have to be eliminated on the railroad because of the tenuous financial condition. This tax relief is to be accomplished through the sale of the L& BR to the IDA for a nominal price, and the leasing back of the railroad to the Group as agent for the operation of the rail line.

Throughout this period IDA members were most instrumental in helping to arrange the creative financing and corporate structures needed for a Payment in Lieu of Taxes (PILOT) program. Though such a PILOT program meant a nearly $50,000 per year property tax loss to various municipalities served by the line, this type of ownership was a far better economic plan for the county and its business climate than outright abandonment and no taxes on a dismantled railroad!

Particularly helpful in developing the aspects of this plan were IDA chairman Urban Karcher, retired Lewis County treasurer, and Christine "Tina" Balash, then the IDA's capable executive director.

A little over a year from the time trains ceased to run on the L&BR, Lansing had invested in it and in the MA&N, obtaining his ten percent interest in each. This meant that the Shay No. 8 would run on the rails of the "new" L&BR.

The line passed to its new operators Wednesday, January 30, 1991!

Rebirth of a Short Line

The line was on the move again; its rebirth nothing short of miraculous. In the days and weeks ahead, there would be new ownership and employees, renewed maintenance and improved carloadings. There was even a steam locomotive on the property. All this, and more, marked the progress on the Lowville & Beaver River line in the early 1990s.

This was accomplished, not surprisingly, through active cooperation, much hard work, and a monetary investment by motivated people.

Some major players in the line's renaissance were not even Lewis County residents when this latest chapter in the line's history unfolded. Some of them have since relocated locally, to help make the railroad's operation a success.

The Wednesday, February 6, 1991 issue of the Lowville *Journal & Republican* was historically significant. Editor and community booster Gordon H. Allen's front page bannered the rebirth of Lewis County's only short line, proclaiming:

Number 1950 heading up freight run on L&BR. (*Courtesy of Maurice Switzer*)

LOWVILLE & BEAVER RIVER RAIL PURCHASED
Genesee Valley Transportation Plans to Have L&BR Operational by the End of the Week

The Genesee Valley Transportation is comprised of investors from the Rochester area: David J. Monte Verde, president; Jeffrey P. Baxter, senior vice president of operations; Charles J. Reidmiller, treasurer and vice president of marketing; Michael D. Thomas, vice president of development; and John S. Herbrand, secretary and general counsel.

Urban Karcher, chairman of the board of directors of the IDA, noted that the IDA felt strongly that the preservation of rail service in Lewis County will benefit its residents and the existing industrial and agricultural base.

Even as Specialty Paperboard and GVT closed the sale on Thursday, vice president of marketing Charles Reidmiller was working with the paper mill's traffic manager to begin the in-bound shipments of alum, latex and waste fibers. The mill has informed the railroad that they will be shipping outbound loads of finished products to their two new customers. This will be the first time in fifteen years the L&BR has handled outbound commodities.

Shay No. 8, in several large pieces, is delivered by "low-boy" truck to Lowville. (*Courtesy of Peter Gores*)

The L&BR management is anxious to restart rail service to the Beaver Falls mills. They feel that the rail service will provide the mills a competitive advantage in these recessionary times.

The L&BR's board of directors is comprised of the five principals of GVT, Baxter, Herbrand, Monte Verde, Reidmiller, Thomas, and Peter Gores. Also on board is Livingston Lansing, Edward Schnabl and Olivia Shoemaker, all residents of Boonville.

The rail officials felt that with turntables at both ends of the line and a nearly 22-mile round trip between Lowville and Croghan, the short line is a natural attraction railroad.

In the days and weeks which followed, GVT worked feverishly to restore the line, not only to previous standards, but in some new directions as well.

At one P.M. on March 3, 1991, Jeff Baxter and Pete Gores, aided by Dan Bogden, opened the throttle on No. 1950 of the L&BR, proceeding northwest from the Lowville yard toward the Conrail interchange of New Bremen, Beaver Falls, and Croghan.

It actually had taken six weeks to restart operations by March 14, 1991. Then, as carloads to and from the mills in Beaver Falls returned to the L&BR's trackage, GVT looked forward to assuming operation of the 16.4-mile Lowville Industrial Track to Carthage and the 46.4-mile Carthage-Newton Falls (and Star Lake) branch. The planned takeover of the 44.8-mile Utica-Lyons Falls Conrail branch was to be delayed until the fall of 1992.

Though the MA&N expansion north of Lowville had been held up, Conrail service was extended to allow the re-born short line to serve its industrial and farm supply customers.

Throughout April 1991, residents of Croghan and Beaver Falls began working on three public celebrations. The first, the Village of Croghan Sesquicentennial was planned for the weekend of May 11 and 12, 1991; the second was the annual Croghan Maple Fest, sponsored by the American Maple Museum; and the third event—central to our account—was the first group of public excursions on the Lowville & Beaver River in many decades.

It was a bright spring day the station had been handsomely repainted in a striking maroon and yellow color scheme, and a bold "Croghan Sesqui" sign adorned one end of the old station building. Besides the customary ticket booth and waiting room, complete with old-time rail posters, the large adjoining freight storage area housed a temporary local rail museum and history center. Displays of old-time rail and farm artifacts, newspaper clippings and even photos from previous editions of this

Hundreds of local residents and out-of-area visitors rode the Croghan to Beaver Falls "excursion shuttle" when passenger rides resumed, after many years' absence, in 1991. (*Courtesy of Maurice Switzer*)

book were on public view.

Number 1950, the now-venerable GE 44-tonner, pulled a rusty but serviceable former Conrail caboose and a silver-sided streamlined coach. The coach, originally on the Richmond, Fredricksburg & Potomac Railroad, was leased from the Central New York Chapter of the National Railway Historical Society in Syracuse.

Later that same day another passenger car addition to the line's roster, former Canadian National Montreal area commuter coach No. 4970, was delivered to the L&BR interchange. The 1950 diesel returned to Lowville and picked up the new arrival.

In the summer of 1991, use of these larger "main line" locomotives between Lowville, Carthage, and Newton Falls caused the MA&N to rebuild the Lowville engine-house for use as a maintenance center. The floor was dug out, lowered, and re-poured with a concrete maintenance pit complete with built-in jacks for heavy repair work.

Not only did thousands of Lewis County residents ride the revived L&BR during the summer and fall of 1991, but many discovered that railroads and their history and operation could be a great hobby for young and old alike.

Accordingly, this high degree of community interest later resulted in formation of a new Railway Historical Society of Northern New York, Inc. headed by Robert Hoffman, as president. The chapter, which has helped support L&BR/MA&N excursions and other activities, worked with governmental and historical groups to form a Lewis County Rail Museum slated to be located in Croghan, near the L&BR tracks.

During the Woodsmen's Field Days in September 1991, at Croghan, a total of eighteen well-patronized trips were conducted. By this time the former RF&P No. 804 and CN commuter coach No. 4970 were joined by another L&BR-based former CN commuter car, No. 5038, owned by Ted Miller, a western New York railfan and GVT management associate specializing in passenger operations.

During a fall excursion schedule over the L&BR, the No. 1950 developed mechanical trouble on Limekiln Hill, north of Lowville. The big C425, No. 806, was very carefully pressed into service on the light L&BR rails. Pete Gores recalls that first it was used to rescue the errant No. 1950. Then Jeff Baxter, Pete and crew made an unprecedented passenger run to Croghan. Though there were some anxious moments among the crew, as the No. 806 was coaxed over the light rail and several turn-of-the-century bridges on the line, the entire episode passed without further problems. The No. 806 drew plenty of attention from Croghan residents and visitors alike, when it remained parked in the little yard there overnight.

Writer and Syracuse, New York newsman, Jeff Paston, commented in the October 1991 issue of *Railroad Model Craftsman* magazine:

> With the L&BR shut down, there was talk that Conrail might abandon its line between Carthage and Low-

Proud owner of Shay No. 8 was Livingston Lansing of Boonville. "Liv" and his wife, Irene, are shown outside his business office the day the Shay was trucked through Boonville on its way from Rome Locomotive Works to the L&BR in Lowville. (*Courtesy of Ed Schnabl*)

ville, further isolating the area from rail transportation. Were it not for Livingston Lansing, a prominent local businessman in nearby Boonville, this might have been the case.

Time, money, and talent were being used to bring the Shay back to prime operating condition and decisions had to be made. Thus, in early October of 1991, the Shay, in several large pieces, was "low-boyed" once again, up over

Impressive even when standing still is Shay No. 8, steamed up for the 1992 Railfan Day at L&BR. At the controls of the geared locomotive is Pete Gores, L&BR general manager. (*Courtesy of Jack Sweeney*)

Town of Croghan historian, Jack Sweeney, snapped this classic view of Shay No. 8 with its consist of former CN commuter cars in June 1992. (*Courtesy of Jack Sweeney*)

the Tug Hill Plateau to its intended home base in Lowville.

G. Robert "Rob" Mangels, formerly associated with the Rome Locomotive Works, and an expert in repairing and restoring steam locomotives, was hired by Liv Lansing to, literally, put the Shay back together.

Fall passenger runs on the "new" L&BR in 1991 were unique. On Saturday, October 19, the 8 A.M. train with No. 1950 ran to Croghan and back before noon.

Following an auto trip to Carthage, made necessary by the poor track conditions on the former Lowville Industrial Track, the afternoon run took place. This was powered by one of the Alco C425's and did not return to Carthage until evening. This unprecedented two-railroad outing was sponsored by the Central New York Chapter NRHS and was the first of its type over these two lines.

The "little geared engine the *almost* could" was on center stage—the L&BR turntable—thanks to an unbelievable amount of hard work and ingenuity by Rob Mangels and his crew: John Pesarek, Robert Hoffman, Kelly Record, Karl Reutling, Paul Kennedy, and Pete Gores on November 16, 1991.

On that cloudy but auspicious fall day, Liv Lansing blew the whistle on old No. 8! The vintage Lima provided the passenger car with live steam heat, and No. 8's air pumps clanked and chugged away—on a stationary basis. Several hundred residents, personally invited by Lansing, then toured the "new" L&BR.

Number 1950 pulled the special to Croghan and back. Uniformed waitresses and staff served delicious hot and cold snacks and other refreshments. Despite cold, dreary weather it was a very nice ride.

An estimated two hundred Lewis County residents, rail employees, volunteers, shippers, suppliers, and friends of Liv Lansing were present for this memorable occasion.

The next vital development came on June 13, 1992. Using three sizable Alco C425-model diesels, (originally from the old Erie-Lackawanna, more recently from British Columbia Rail) the MA&N began Lowville-Carthage and Carthage-Newton Falls revenue freight runs. The L&BR's connection with the nation's rail system at large had been secured. However, transfer of the Lyons Falls trackage was put on hold until September 1992.

As a result, the No. 1950 has sometimes been operated as far north as Carthage to help with yard-switching there. Originally, two of the big MA&N Alcos were parked at the Carthage yard, with one in reserve at Lowville.

June 13 and 14, 1992 was the L&BR's First Annual Railfan Weekend. Excursions that included photo stops and run-bys were made during the day and spectacular night photo sessions were also staged.

A number of other special excursions were made by the MA&N/L&BR that summer and fall. This basic pattern was continued during the summer and fall of 1992, which presented the line to the public as a modest local freight-hauler and periodic excursion operator.

The troubles with No. 8's truck bearings overheating continued to plague Rob Mangels and his crew throughout 1992. Then, on December 26, 1992, came a truly unfortunate occurrence with the passing away of Liv Lansing, after a lengthy illness. He is sorely missed.

Finally, during the winter of 1993, the offending trucks had their axles and bearings re-machined at Lowville and Carthage.

By the winter of 1994, the Lowville line was reeling from an onslaught of snow. With snow depths reaching as high as eight feet on the Tug Hill Plateau, the road's employees were bracing themselves for the very real possibility of "hundred-year" floods along the Black and Beaver

The Black River Valley during the January flood of 1998. Record-high crests two to four feet over flood stage came close to taking down the two L&BR bridges at "the Flats" near Dadville, just north of Lowville. At top, a view looking east at Illingsworth Bridge crossing. At right, waves lap at ties on the main span across the Black River. Amazingly, neither rail bridge was damaged by the flooding—this time! (*Courtesy of Peter Gores*)

A vintage Russell plow of the L&BR; the cutting edge of rail-borne snow removal, circa 1927. More than a dozen plow runs were made on the Lowville line during the "old-fashioned" winter of 1993. (*Courtesy of Maurice Switzer*)

River watersheds. Thankfully, this did not materialize.

Following what had been a general lack of excursion activity throughout 1993, the L&BR and its local supporters were gratified when, in the winter of 1994, Karl J. Reutling, head of the Lewis County Opportunities office in New Bremen and vice president of the Railway Historical Society of Northern New York, announced that the Shay No. 8, which had been at the L&BR engine house all along, had officially been donated to the local railroad club.

Speaking for that group, and all concerned local "fans" of the railroad, he stated in a January 1994 article in the *Watertown Daily Times* that, "It's a nice retirement for the locomotive." The write-up, by *Times* staffer David A. Smith, revealed that the Railway Historical Society of Northern New York had recently been given the Shay by the late Liv Lansing's estate. Reutling also indicated that the group was "negotiating with James Scanlon, owner of the depot in Croghan" as a prelude to developing that quaint structure as a future museum site and tourist center. Later, an enginehouse was also built for the Shay at Croghan in cooperation with the Lansing estate which generously continues to support the efforts to preserve the Shay No. 8 for posterity.

As the future continues to unfold, the L&BR operates as an integral part of a regional rail operation, not as a truly independent entity. However, for the Lowville & Beaver River, its employees and friends in the rail community, life indeed does go on!

LOCOMOTIVE ROSTER — LOWVILLE & BEAVER RIVER RAILROAD

No.	Builder	Bldr. No.	Type	Year Built	Weight	Cyl & Drivers	Source	Disposition
10	Schenectady	1870	4-4-0				Ex-Adirondack RR #3, "C.F. Durkee"	
12								
51	Schenectady	940	0-4-0	11-1873		15"x22" — 50"	Ex NYC #51	
1912	Alco-Schenectady	51125	4-6-0	4-1912				Apparently sold or scrapped in 1947
1923	Alco-Cooke	62623	2-8-0	3-1923				Sold to Steamtown, USA in 1964
1947	GE	28345	B-B	4-1947	44 tons		Rebuilt in 1954	In alternate service
1950	GE	30461	B-B	6-1950	44 tons		Ex-Louisville & Nashville No. 3101, purchased in 1963.	In alternate service
1951	GE	33706	B-B	1950	44 tons		Originally Skaneateles short line No. 6	
502	Hall-Scott		gas mechanical railcar "jitney"				Ex-Salt Lake & Utah	Scrapped